MznLnx

Missing Links Exam Preps

Exam Prep for

Mathematics: A Practical Odyssey

Johnson & Mowry, 6th Edition

The MznLnx Exam Prep is your link from the texbook and lecture to your exams.
The MznLnx Exam Preps are unauthorized and comprehensive reviews of your textbooks.

All material provided by MznLnx and Rico Publications (c) 2010
Textbook publishers and textbook authors do not particpate in or contribute to these reviews.

MznLnx

Rico
Publications

Exam Prep for Mathematics: A Practical Odyssey
6th Edition
Johnson & Mowry

Publisher: Raymond Houge
Assistant Editor: Michael Rouger
Text and Cover Designer: Lisa Buckner
Marketing Manager: Sara Swagger
Project Manager, Editorial Production: Jerry Emerson
Art Director: Vernon Lowerui

Product Manager: Dave Mason
Editorial Assitant: Rachel Guzmanji
Pedagogy: Debra Long
Cover Image: Jim Reed/Getty Images
Text and Cover Printer: City Printing, Inc.
Compositor: Media Mix, Inc.

(c) 2010 Rico Publications
ALL RIGHTS RESERVED. No part of this work covered by the copyright may be reproduced or used in any form or by an means--graphic, electronic, or mechanical, including photocopying, recording, taping, Web distribution, information storage, and retrieval systems, or in any other manner--without the written permission of the publisher.

Printed in the United States
ISBN:

For more information about our products, contact us at:
Dave.Mason@RicoPublications.com

For permission to use material from this text or product, submit a request online to:
Dave.Mason@RicoPublications.com

Contents

CHAPTER 1
LOGIC   1
CHAPTER 2
SETS AND COUNTING   17
CHAPTER 3
PROBABILITY   28
CHAPTER 4
STATISTICS   38
CHAPTER 5
FINANCE   49
CHAPTER 6
VOTING AND APPORTIONMENT   54
CHAPTER 7
NUMBER SYSTEMS AND NUMBER THEORY   56
CHAPTER 8
GEOMETRY   63
CHAPTER 9
GRAPH THEORY   79
CHAPTER 10
EXPONENTIAL AND LOGARITHMIC FUNCTIONS   86
CHAPTER 11
MATRICES AND MARKOV CHAINS   93
CHAPTER 12
LINEAR PROGRAMMING   99
ANSWER KEY   103

TO THE STUDENT

COMPREHENSIVE

The *MznLnx* Exam Prep series is designed to help you pass your exams. Editors at MznLnx review your textbooks and then prepare these practice exams to help you master the textbook material. Unlike study guides, workbooks, and practice tests provided by the texbook publisher and textbook authors, *MznLnx* gives you **all** of the material in each chapter in exam form, not just samples, so you can be sure to nail your exam.

MECHANICAL

The MznLnx Exam Prep series creates exams that will help you learn the subject matter as well as test you on your understanding. Each question is designed to help you master the concept. Just working through the exams, you gain an understanding of the subject--its a simple mechanical process that produces success.

INTEGRATED STUDY GUIDE AND REVIEW

MznLnx is not just a set of exams designed to test you, its also a comprehensive review of the subject content. Each exam question is also a review of the concept, making sure that you will get the answer correct without having to go to other sources of material. You learn as you go! Its the easiest way to pass an exam.

HUMOR

Studying can be tedious and dry. MznLnx's instructional design includes moderate humor within the exam questions on occassion, to break the tedium and revitalize the brain

Chapter 1. LOGIC

1. A _____ number is a positive integer which has a positive divisor other than one or itself. By definition, every integer greater than one is either a prime number or a _____ number. zero and one are considered to be neither prime nor _____. For example, the integer 14 is a _____ number because it can be factored as 2 × 7.
   - a. Basis
   - b. Key server
   - c. Composite
   - d. Discontinuity

2. A _____ is a positive integer which has a positive divisor other than one or itself. In other words, if 0 < n is an integer and there are integers 1 < a, b < n such that n = a × b then n is composite. By definition, every integer greater than one is either a prime number or a _____.
   - a. Ruth-Aaron pair
   - b. Megaprime
   - c. Prime Pages
   - d. Composite number

3. _____, as that term is used in this article, is the mathematics written in Greek, developed from the 6th century BC to the 5th century AD around the Eastern shores of the Mediterranean. The word 'mathematics' itself derives from the ancient Greek μαθημα, meaning 'subject of instruction'.. The study of mathematics for its own sake and the use of generalized mathematical theories and proofs is the key difference between _____ and those of preceding civilizations.
   - a. 120-cell
   - b. Greek mathematics
   - c. 2-3 heap
   - d. 1-center problem

4. _____ is the study of the principles of valid demonstration and inference. _____ is a branch of philosophy, a part of the classical trivium of grammar, _____, and rhetoric. of λογικῐές, 'possessed of reason, intellectual, dialectical, argumentative', from λῐŒγος logos, 'word, thought, idea, argument, account, reason, or principle'.
   - a. Logic
   - b. Boolean function
   - c. Satisfiability
   - d. Counterpart theory

5. In mathematics, _____ and undefined are used to explain whether or not expressions have meaningful, sensible, and unambiguous values. Not all branches of mathematics come to the same conclusion.

   The following expressions are undefined in all contexts, but remarks in the analysis section may apply.
   - a. Defined
   - b. Plugging in
   - c. Toy model
   - d. LHS

6. Induction or _____, sometimes called inductive logic, is the process of reasoning in which the premises of an argument are believed to support the conclusion but do not entail it;. Induction is a form of reasoning that makes generalizations based on individual instances. It is used to ascribe properties or relations to types based on an observation instance; or to formulate laws based on limited observations of recurring phenomenal patterns.
   - a. Intuitionistic logic
   - b. Affine logic
   - c. Idempotency of entailment
   - d. Inductive reasoning

7. _____ or set diagrams are diagrams that show all hypothetically possible logical relations between a finite collection of sets. _____ were invented around 1880 by John Venn. They are used in many fields, including set theory, probability, logic, statistics, and computer science.
   - a. 1-center problem
   - b. 2-3 heap
   - c. 120-cell
   - d. Venn diagrams

8. A _____ is a device for performing mathematical calculations, distinguished from a computer by having a limited problem solving ability and an interface optimized for interactive calculation rather than programming. _____s can be hardware or software, and mechanical or electronic, and are often built into devices such as PDAs or mobile phones.

Modern electronic _____s are generally small, digital, and usually inexpensive.

   a. Calculator
   b. 2-3 heap
   c. 1-center problem
   d. 120-cell

9. A _____ is a 2D geometric symbolic representation of information according to some visualization technique. Sometimes, the technique uses a 3D visualization which is then projected onto the 2D surface. The word graph is sometimes used as a synonym for _____.

   a. 2-3 heap
   b. 1-center problem
   c. Diagram
   d. 120-cell

10. _____ is the wagering of money or something of material value on an event with an uncertain outcome with the primary intent of winning additional money and/or material goods. Typically, the outcome of the wager is evident within a short period.

The term gaming in this context typically refers to instances in which the activity has been specifically permitted by law.

   a. 1-center problem
   b. 2-3 heap
   c. 120-cell
   d. Gambling

11. A _____ typically refers to a class of handheld calculators that are capable of plotting graphs, solving simultaneous equations, and performing numerous other tasks with variables. Most popular _____s are also programmable, allowing the user to create customized programs, typically for scientific/engineering and education applications. Due to their large displays intended for graphing, they can also accommodate several lines of text and calculations at a time.

   a. Genus
   b. Support vector machines
   c. Bump mapping
   d. Graphing calculator

12. In statistics, _____ is a form of regression analysis in which the relationship between one or more independent variables and another variable, called dependent variable, is modeled by a least squares function, called _____ equation. This function is a linear combination of one or more model parameters, called regression coefficients. A _____ equation with one independent variable represents a straight line.

   a. Kurtosis
   b. Percentile rank
   c. Linear regression
   d. Random variables

13. A quadratic equation with real solutions, called roots, which may be real or complex, is given by the _____: $x = \frac{-b \pm \sqrt{b^2 - 4ac}}{2a}$.

   a. Quadratic formula
   b. Differential Algebra
   c. Quotient
   d. Parametric continuity

Chapter 1. LOGIC

14. _____ is a quantity expressing the two-dimensional size of a defined part of a surface, typically a region bounded by a closed curve. The term surface _____ refers to the total _____ of the exposed surface of a 3-dimensional solid, such as the sum of the _____s of the exposed sides of a polyhedron. _____ is an important invariant in the differential geometry of surfaces.
    a. A chemical equation
    b. A Mathematical Theory of Communication
    c. A posteriori
    d. Area

15. In mathematics, a _____ is a constant multiplicative factor of a certain object. For example, in the expression $9x^2$, the _____ of x^2 is 9.

The object can be such things as a variable, a vector, a function, etc.

    a. Multivariate division algorithm
    b. Coefficient
    c. Stability radius
    d. Fibonacci polynomials

16. In probability theory and statistics, _____ indicates the strength and direction of a linear relationship between two random variables. That is in contrast with the usage of the term in colloquial speech, denoting any relationship, not necessarily linear. In general statistical usage, _____ or co-relation refers to the departure of two random variables from independence.
    a. Sample size
    b. Correlation
    c. Random variables
    d. Summary statistics

17. In mathematics and in the sciences, a _____ (plural: _____e, formulæ or _____s) is a concise way of expressing information symbolically (as in a mathematical or chemical _____), or a general relationship between quantities. One of many famous _____e is Albert Einstein's $E = mc^2$ (see special relativity

In mathematics, a _____ is a key to solve an equation with variables. For example, the problem of determining the volume of a sphere is one that requires a significant amount of integral calculus to solve.

    a. Formula
    b. 120-cell
    c. 2-3 heap
    d. 1-center problem

18. The _____ fallacy is an informal fallacy. It ascribes cause where none exists. The flaw is failing to account for natural fluctuations.
    a. Regression
    b. Degrees of freedom
    c. Differential
    d. Depth

19. A _____ is one of the basic shapes of geometry: a polygon with three corners or vertices and three sides or edges which are line segments. A _____ with vertices A, B, and C is denoted ABC.

In Euclidean geometry any three non-collinear points determine a unique _____ and a unique plane.

    a. Fuhrmann circle
    b. Kepler triangle
    c. 1-center problem
    d. Triangle

Chapter 1. LOGIC

20. _____ is a branch of mathematics that includes the study of limits, derivatives, integrals, and infinite series, and constitutes a major part of modern university education. Historically, it has been referred to as 'the _____ of infinitesimals', or 'infinitesimal _____'. Most basically, _____ is the study of change, in the same way that geometry is the study of space.

   a. Hyperbolic angle
   b. Partial sum
   c. Test for Divergence
   d. Calculus

21. A _____ is a mathematical table used in logic -- specifically in connection with Boolean algebra, boolean functions, and propositional calculus -- to compute the functional values of logical expressions on each of their functional arguments, that is, on each combination of values taken by their logical variables. In particular, _____s can be used to tell whether a propositional expression is true for all legitimate input values, that is, logically valid.

The pattern of reasoning that the _____ tabulates was Frege's, Peirce's, and Schröder's by 1880.

   a. 1-center problem
   b. 120-cell
   c. Truth table
   d. 2-3 heap

22. A _____ is a software program that facilitates symbolic mathematics. The core functionality of a CAS is manipulation of mathematical expressions in symbolic form.

Chapter 1. LOGIC

The symbolic manipulations supported typically include

- simplification to the smallest possible expression or some standard form, including automatic simplification with assumptions and simplification with constraints
- substitution of symbolic, functors or numeric values for expressions
- change of form of expressions: expanding products and powers, partial and full factorization, rewriting as partial fractions, constraint satisfaction, rewriting trigonometric functions as exponentials, etc.
- partial and total differentiation
- symbolic constrained and unconstrained global optimization
- solution of linear and some non-linear equations over various domains
- solution of some differential and difference equations
- taking some limits
- some indefinite and definite integration, including multidimensional integrals
- integral transforms
- arbitrary-precision numeric operations
- Series operations such as expansion, summation and products
- matrix operations including products, inverses, etc.
- display of mathematical expressions in two-dimensional mathematical form, often using typesetting systems similar to TeX
- add-ons for use in applied mathematics such as physics packages for physical computation
- plotting graphs and parametric plots of functions in two and three dimensions, and animating them
- APIs for linking it on an external program such as a database, or using in a programming language to use the _____
- drawing charts and diagrams
- string manipulation such as matching and searching
- statistical computation
- Theorem proving and verification
- graphic production and editing such as CGI and signal processing as image processing
- sound synthesis

Many also include a programming language, allowing users to implement their own algorithms.

Some _____s focus on a specific area of application; these are typically developed in academia and are free.

a. 120-cell
c. 2-3 heap
b. 1-center problem
d. Computer algebra system

23. _____ Galilei (15 February 1564 - 8 January 1642) was a Tuscan physicist, mathematician, astronomer, and philosopher who played a major role in the Scientific Revolution. His achievements include improvements to the telescope and consequent astronomical observations, and support for Copernicanism. _____ has been called the 'father of modern observational astronomy', the 'father of modern physics', the 'father of science', and 'the Father of Modern Science.' The motion of uniformly accelerated objects, taught in nearly all high school and introductory college physics courses, was studied by _____ as the subject of kinematics.

Chapter 1. LOGIC

a. Francesco Severi
b. Galileo
c. David Naccache
d. Jan Kowalewski

24. In linear algebra, _____ is a version of Gaussian elimination that puts zeros both above and below each pivot element as it goes from the top row of the given matrix to the bottom. In other words, _____ brings a matrix to reduced row echelon form, whereas Gaussian elimination takes it only as far as row echelon form. Every matrix has a reduced row echelon form, and this algorithm is guaranteed to produce it.

a. Conservation form
b. Gauss-Jordan elimination
c. Spheroidal wave functions
d. Lax equivalence theorem

25. In mathematics, _____ is a technique for optimization of a linear objective function, subject to linear equality and linear inequality constraints. Informally, _____ determines the way to achieve the best outcome in a given mathematical model given some list of requirements represented as linear equations.

More formally, given a polytope, and a real-valued affine function

$$f(x_1, x_2, \ldots, x_n) = c_1 x_1 + c_2 x_2 + \cdots + c_n x_n + d$$

defined on this polytope, a _____ method will find a point in the polytope where this function has the smallest value.

a. Linear programming relaxation
b. Lin-Kernighan
c. Descent direction
d. Linear programming

26. In mathematics, a _____, named after Andrey Markov, is a stochastic process with the Markov property. Having the Markov property means that, given the present state, future states are independent of the past states. In other words, the description of the present state fully captures all the information that could influence the future evolution of the process. Future states will be reached through a probabilistic process instead of a deterministic one.

a. Markov chain
b. Variance-to-mean ratio
c. Possibility theory
d. Law of Truly Large Numbers

27. In geometry, a _____ or n-_____ is an n-dimensional analogue of a triangle. Specifically, a _____ is the convex hull of a set of affinely independent points in some Euclidean space of dimension n or higher.

For example, a 0-_____ is a point, a 1-_____ is a line segment, a 2-_____ is a triangle, a 3-_____ is a tetrahedron, and a 4-_____ is a pentachoron.

a. Demihypercubes
b. Hypercell
c. Polytetrahedron
d. Simplex

28. In mathematical optimization theory, the simplex algorithm, created by the American mathematician George Dantzig in 1947, is a popular algorithm for numerical solution of the linear programming problem. The journal Computing in Science and Engineering listed it as one of the top 10 algorithms of the century.

Chapter 1. LOGIC

An unrelated, but similarly named method is the Nelder-Mead method or downhill _____ due to Nelder ' Mead and is a numerical method for optimising many-dimensional unconstrained problems, belonging to the more general class of search algorithms.

a. Fibonacci search
c. Hill climbing
b. Simplex method
d. Differential evolution

29. In Linear programming a _____ is a variable which is added to a constraint to turn the inequality into an equation. This is required to turn an inequality into an equality where a linear combination of variables is less than or equal to a given constant in the former. As with the other variables in the augmented constraints, the _____ cannot take on negative values, as the Simplex algorithm requires them to be positive or zero.

a. Shekel function
c. Bellman equation
b. Shape optimization
d. Slack variable

30. _____ or amortisation is the process of decreasing an amount over a period of time. The word comes from Middle English amortisen to kill, alienate in mortmain, from Anglo-French amorteser, alteration of amortir, from Vulgar Latin admortire to kill, from Latin ad- + mort-, mors death. Particular instances of the term include:

- _____, the allocation of a lump sum amount to different time periods, particularly for loans and other forms of finance, including related interest or other finance charges.
    - _____ schedule, a table detailing each periodic payment on a loan, as generated by an _____ calculator.
    - Negative _____, an _____ schedule where the loan amount actually increases through not paying the full interest
- Amortized analysis, analyzing the execution cost of algorithms over a sequence of operations.
- _____ of capital expenditures of certain assets under accounting rules, particularly intangible assets, in a manner analogous to depreciation.
- _____

_____ is also used in the context of zoning regulations and describes the time in which a property owner has to relocate when the property's use constitutes a preexisting nonconforming use under zoning regulations.

- Depreciation

a. Identity
c. ISAAC
b. Origin
d. Amortization

31. An _____ is a table detailing each periodic payment on a amortizing loan, as generated by an amortization calculator.

While a portion of every payment is applied towards both the interest and the principal balance of the loan, the exact amount applied to principal each time varies. An _____ reveals the specific monetary amount put towards interest, as well as the specific put towards the Principal balance, with each payment.

a. A Mathematical Theory of Communication
b. A chemical equation
c. Accounts receivable
d. Amortization schedule

32. In mathematics, hyperbolic n-space, denoted H^n, is the maximally symmetric, simply connected, n-dimensional Riemannian manifold with constant sectional curvature −1. _____ is the principal example of a space exhibiting hyperbolic geometry. It can be thought of as the negative-curvature analogue of the n-sphere.
   a. Margulis lemma
   b. Hyperbolic geometry
   c. Hyperbolic space
   d. Horocycle

33. In mathematics, a _____ is a rectangular table of elements, which may be numbers or, more generally, any abstract quantities that can be added and multiplied. Matrices are used to describe linear equations, keep track of the coefficients of linear transformations and to record data that depend on multiple parameters. Matrices are described by the field of _____ theory.
   a. Double counting
   b. Coherent
   c. Compression
   d. Matrix

34. _____ is the mathematical operation of scaling one number by another. It is one of the four basic operations in elementary arithmetic.

_____ is defined for whole numbers in terms of repeated addition; for example, 4 multiplied by 3 can be calculated by adding 3 copies of 4 together:

$$4 + 4 + 4 = 12.$$

_____ of rational numbers and real numbers is defined by systematic generalization of this basic idea.

   a. Highest common factor
   b. The number 0 is even.
   c. Least common multiple
   d. Multiplication

35. In abstract algebra, a module S over a ring R is called _____ or irreducible if it is not the zero module 0 and if its only submodules are 0 and S. Understanding the _____ modules over a ring is usually helpful because these modules form the 'building blocks' of all other modules in a certain sense.

Abelian groups are the same as Z-modules.

   a. Simple
   b. Harmonic series
   c. Basis
   d. Derivation

36. _____ is the path of a moving object that it follows through space. The object might be a projectile or a satellite, for example. It thus includes the meaning of orbit - the path of a planet, an asteroid or a comet as it travels around a central mass.
   a. 1-center problem
   b. Trajectory
   c. Trajectory optimization
   d. 120-cell

37. In complex analysis, a branch of mathematics, the _____ of a complex-valued function g is a function whose complex derivative is g. More precisely, given an open set U in the complex plane and a function $g: U \to \mathbb{C}$, the _____ of g is a function $f: U \to \mathbb{C}$ that satisfies $\frac{df}{dz} = g$.

As such, this concept is the complex-variable version of the _____ of a real-valued function.

   a. Integration by parts
   b. Integral
   c. Indefinite integral
   d. Antiderivative

38. In mathematics, an _____, or central tendency of a data set refers to a measure of the 'middle' or 'expected' value of the data set. There are many different descriptive statistics that can be chosen as a measurement of the central tendency of the data items.

An _____ is a single value that is meant to typify a list of values.

   a. A chemical equation
   b. A posteriori
   c. A Mathematical Theory of Communication
   d. Average

39. _____ (October 1630 - 4 May 1677) was an English scholar and mathematician who is generally given credit for his early role in the development of calculus; in particular, for the discovery of the fundamental theorem of calculus. His work centered on the properties of the tangent; Barrow was the first to calculate the tangents of the kappa curve. Isaac Newton was a student of Barrow's, and Newton went on to develop calculus in a modern form.
   a. Abraham Sinkov
   b. Adi Shamir
   c. Agnes Meyer Driscoll
   d. Isaac Barrow

40. _____ was a French mathematician. He started the project of formulating and proving the theorems of infinitesimal calculus in a rigorous manner and was thus an early pioneer of analysis. He also gave several important theorems in complex analysis and initiated the study of permutation groups.
   a. Edward Kofler
   b. Adi Shamir
   c. Alston Scott Householder
   d. Augustin Louis Cauchy

41. In mathematics, the concept of a _____ tries to capture the intuitive idea of a geometrical one-dimensional and continuous object. A simple example is the circle. In everyday use of the term '_____', a straight line is not curved, but in mathematical parlance _____s include straight lines and line segments.
   a. Negative pedal curve
   b. Quadrifolium
   c. Kappa curve
   d. Curve

42. _____ is a fundamental construction of differential calculus and admits many possible generalizations within the fields of mathematical analysis, combinatorics, algebra, and geometry.

In real, complex, and functional analysis, _____s are generalized to functions of several real or complex variables and functions between topological vector spaces. An important case is the variational _____ in the calculus of variations.

a. Metric derivative
b. Functional derivative
c. Lin-Tsien equation
d. Derivative

43. In mathematics, an _____ or member of a set is any one of the distinct objects that make up that set.

Writing A = {1,2,3,4}, means that the _____s of the set A are the numbers 1, 2, 3 and 4. Groups of _____s of A, for example {1,2}, are subsets of A.

a. Ideal
b. Element
c. Universal code
d. Order

44. _____ IPA: [pjɛː ɛ dɛ™fɛː 'ma] (17 August 1601 or 1607/8 - 12 January 1665) was a French lawyer at the Parlement of Toulouse, France, and a mathematician who is given credit for early developments that led to modern calculus. In particular, he is recognized for his discovery of an original method of finding the greatest and the smallest ordinates of curved lines, which is analogous to that of the then unknown differential calculus, as well as his research into the theory of numbers. He also made notable contributions to analytic geometry, probability, and optics.

a. Philip J. Davis
b. Pierre de Fermat
c. Felix Hausdorff
d. Nikita Borisov

45. In mathematics, a _____ is traditionally a map from a vector space to the field underlying the vector space, which is usually the real numbers. In other words, it is a function that takes a vector as its argument or input and returns a scalar. Its use goes back to the calculus of variations where one searches for a function which minimizes a certain _____.

a. Functional
b. Curl
c. Derivation
d. Kernel

46. _____s have been used to express the idea of objects so small that there is no way to see them or to measure them. For everyday life, an _____ object is an object which is smaller than any possible measure. When used as an adjective in the vernacular, '_____' means extremely small, but not necessarily 'infinitely small'.

a. Infinitesimal
b. A Mathematical Theory of Communication
c. A posteriori
d. A chemical equation

47. In cryptography, _____ is a pseudorandom number generator and a stream cipher designed by Robert Jenkins to be cryptographically secure. The name is an acronym for Indirection, Shift, Accumulate, Add, and Count.

The _____ algorithm has similarities with RC4.

a. Introduction
b. Order
c. Imputation
d. Isaac

48. _____ was a German polymath who wrote primarily in Latin and French.

He occupies an equally grand place in both the history of philosophy and the history of mathematics. He invented infinitesimal calculus independently of Newton, and his notation is the one in general use since then.

Chapter 1. LOGIC

a. Raymond Merrill Smullyan	b. Harry Hinsley
c. Michel Rolle	d. Gottfried Wilhelm Leibniz

49. The _____ (symbol: N) is the SI derived unit of force, named after Isaac _____ in recognition of his work on classical mechanics.

The _____ is the unit of force derived in the SI system; it is equal to the amount of force required to accelerate a mass of one kilogram at a rate of one meter per second per second. Algebraically:

$$1\ N = 1\ \frac{kg \cdot m}{s^2}.$$

- 1 N is the force of Earth's gravity on an object with a mass of about 102 g ($\frac{1}{9.8}$ kg) (such as a small apple.)
- On Earth's surface, a mass of 1 kg exerts a force of approximately 9.80665 N [down] (or 1 kgf.) The approximation of 1 kg corresponding to 10 N is sometimes used as a rule of thumb in everyday life and in engineering.
- The force of Earth's gravity on a human being with a mass of 70 kg is approximately 687 N.
- The dot product of force and distance is mechanical work. Thus, in SI units, a force of 1 N exerted over a distance of 1 m is 1 NÂ·m of work. The Work-Energy Theorem states that the work done on a body is equal to the change in energy of the body. 1 NÂ·m = 1 J (joule), the SI unit of energy.
- It is common to see forces expressed in kilonewtons or kN, where 1 kN = 1 000 N.

a. Newton	b. 1-center problem
c. 120-cell	d. 2-3 heap

50. In mathematics, the _____ is a conic section, the intersection of a right circular conical surface and a plane parallel to a generating straight line of that surface. Given a point and a line that lie in a plane, the locus of points in that plane that are equidistant to them is a _____.

A particular case arises when the plane is tangent to the conical surface of a circle.

a. Dandelin sphere	b. Directrix
c. Parabola	d. Matrix representation of conic sections

51. _____ is a special mathematical relationship between two quantities.Two quantities are called proportional if they vary in such a way that one of the quantities is a constant multiple of the other, or equivalently if they have a constant ratio.
a. Depth	b. Compression
c. Discontinuity	d. Proportionality

Chapter 1. LOGIC

52. A _____ is a building where the upper surfaces are triangular and converge on one point. The base of _____s are usually quadrilateral or trilateral, meaning that a _____ usually has four or five faces. A _____'s design, with the majority of the weight closer to the ground, means that less material higher up on the _____ will be pushing down from above.
   a. 1-center problem
   b. 120-cell
   c. Pyramid
   d. 2-3 heap

53. _____ is a term in mathematics. It can refer to:

   - a _____ line, in geometry
   - the trigonometric function called _____
   - the _____ method, a root-finding algorithm in numerical analysis

   a. Solvable
   b. Separable
   c. Large set
   d. Secant

54. _____ is used to describe the steepness, incline, gradient, or grade of a straight line. A higher _____ value indicates a steeper incline. The _____ is defined as the ratio of the 'rise' divided by the 'run' between two points on a line, or in other words, the ratio of the altitude change to the horizontal distance between any two points on the line.
   a. Cognitively Guided Instruction
   b. Point plotting
   c. Number line
   d. Slope

55. In trigonometry, the _____ is a function defined as $\tan x = \sin x / \cos x$. The function is so-named because it can be defined as the length of a certain segment of a _____ (in the geometric sense) to the unit circle. In plane geometry, a line is _____ to a curve, at some point, if both line and curve pass through the point with the same direction.
   a. Tangent
   b. Conformal geometry
   c. Projective connection
   d. Hopf conjectures

56. In geometry, the _____ to a curve at a given point is the straight line that 'just touches' the curve at that point. As it passes through the point of tangency, the _____ is 'going in the same direction' as the curve, and in this sense it is the best straight-line approximation to the curve at that point. The same definition applies to space curves and curves in n-dimensional Euclidean space.
   a. Four-vertex theorem
   b. Darboux frame
   c. Chern-Weil theory
   d. Tangent line

57. In geometry, a _____ is a special kind of point, usually a corner of a polygon, polyhedron, or higher dimensional polytope. In the geometry of curves a _____ is a point of where the first derivative of curvature is zero. In graph theory, a _____ is the fundamental unit out of which graphs are formed
   a. Duality
   b. Vertex
   c. Dini
   d. Crib

58. The mathematical concept of a _____ expresses the intuitive idea of deterministic dependence between two quantities, one of which is viewed as primary and the other as secondary. A _____ then is a way to associate a unique output for each input of a specified type, for example, a real number or an element of a given set.

Chapter 1. LOGIC

a. Coherent	b. Going up
c. Grill	d. Function

59. An _____ is an increase of some amount, either fixed or variable. For example one's salary may have a fixed annual _____ or one based on a percentage of its current value. A decrease is called a decrement.

a. Increment	b. A posteriori
c. A Mathematical Theory of Communication	d. A chemical equation

60. In mathematics, the _____ is an approach to finding a particular solution to certain inhomogeneous ordinary differential equations and recurrence relations. It is closely related to the annihilator method, but instead of using a particular kind of differential operator in order to find the best possible form of the particular solution, a 'guess' is made as to the appropriate form, which is then tested by differentiating the resulting equation. In this sense, the _____ is less formal but more intuitive than the annihilator method.

a. Phase line	b. Linear differential equation
c. Method of undetermined coefficients	d. Differential algebraic equations

61. In microeconomics, _____ is the term used to refer to total when marginal cost is subtracted from marginal revenue. Under the marginal approach to profit maximization, to maximize profits, a firm should continue to produce a good until _____ is zero. Profit Maximization - The Marginal Approach

{{Economics-stub}}

a. 1-center problem	b. Marginal profit
c. 120-cell	d. 2-3 heap

62. The _____ of an object located in some space refers to the part of space occupied by the object as determined by its external boundary -- abstracting from other aspects the object may have such as its colour, content as well as from the object's position and orientation in space, and its size.

According to famous mathematician and statistician David George Kendall, _____ may be defined as

Simple two-dimensional _____s can be described by basic geometry such as points, line, curves, plane, and so on. _____s that occur in the physical world are often quite complex; they may be arbitrarily curved as studied by differential geometry as for plants or coastlines.)

a. Spidron	b. Shape
c. Confocal	d. Parallel lines

63. In linear algebra, two n-by-n matrices A and B over the field K are called _____ if there exists an invertible n-by-n matrix P over K such that

$$P^{-1}AP = B.$$

One of the meanings of the term similarity transformation is such a transformation of a matrix A into a matrix B.

Similarity is an equivalence relation on the space of square matrices.

_____ matrices share many properties:

- rank
- determinant
- trace
- eigenvalues
- characteristic polynomial
- minimal polynomial
- elementary divisors

There are two reasons for these facts:

- two _____ matrices can be thought of as describing the same linear map, but with respect to different bases
- the map $X \mapsto P^{-1}XP$ is an automorphism of the associative algebra of all n-by-n matrices, as the one-object case of the above category of all matrices.

Because of this, for a given matrix A, one is interested in finding a simple 'normal form' B which is _____ to A -- the study of A then reduces to the study of the simpler matrix B.

a. Coherence
b. Blinding
c. Dense
d. Similar

64. _____ generally conveys two primary meanings. The first is an imprecise sense of harmonious or aesthetically-pleasing proportionality and balance; such that it reflects beauty or perfection. The second meaning is a precise and well-defined concept of balance or 'patterned self-similarity' that can be demonstrated or proved according to the rules of a formal system: by geometry, through physics or otherwise.

a. Symmetry breaking
b. Tessellation
c. Molecular symmetry
d. Symmetry

65. The _____ of any solid, plasma, vacuum or theoretical object is how much three-dimensional space it occupies, often quantified numerically. One-dimensional figures and two-dimensional shapes are assigned zero _____ in the three-dimensional space. _____ is presented as ml or cm^3.

_____s of straight-edged and circular shapes are calculated using arithmetic formulae.

a. Cauchy momentum equation
b. Stress-energy tensor
c. Volume
d. Thermodynamic limit

Chapter 1. LOGIC

66. In logic, two sentences (either in a formal language or a natural language) may be joined by means of a _____ to form a compound sentence. The truth-value of the compound is uniquely determined by the truth-values of the simpler sentences. The _____ therefore represents a function, and since the value of the compound sentence is a truth-value, it is called a truth-function and the _____ is called a 'truth-functional connective'.
- a. Set theory
- b. Logical connective
- c. Satisfiability
- d. Fallacies of definition

67. In logic and mathematics, _____ or not is an operation on logical values, for example, the logical value of a proposition, that sends true to false and false to true. Intuitively, the _____ of a proposition holds exactly when that proposition does not hold. In grammar, nor is an adverb which acts as a coordinating conjunction.
- a. 1-center problem
- b. Sentence diagram
- c. Syntax
- d. Negation

68. In logic and mathematics, or, also known as logical _____ or inclusive _____ is a logical operator that results in true whenever one or more of its operands are true. In grammar, or is a coordinating conjunction. In ordinary language 'or' rather has the meaning of exclusive _____.
- a. Zero-point energy
- b. Triquetra
- c. Cube
- d. Disjunction

69. An _____ is one that cannot be compressed because it lacks sufficient repeating sequences. Whether a string is compressible will often depend on the algorithm being used. Some examples may illuminate this.
- a. Arithmetic coding
- b. Incompressible string
- c. A Mathematical Theory of Communication
- d. Entropy encoding

70. In the study of metric spaces in mathematics, there are various notions of two metrics on the same underlying space being 'the same', or _____.

In the following, M will denote a non-empty set and d_1 and d_2 will denote two metrics on M.

The two metrics d_1 and d_2 are said to be topologically _____ if they generate the same topology on M.

- a. Equivalent
- b. A Mathematical Theory of Communication
- c. A posteriori
- d. A chemical equation

71. In propositional logic, contraposition is a logical relationship between two statements of material implication. A proposition Q is materially implicated by a proposition P when the following relationship holds:

$$(P \rightarrow Q)$$

In vernacular terms, this states 'If P then Q', or, 'If Socrates is a man then Socrates is human.' In a conditional such as this, P is called the antecedent and Q the consequent. One statement is the _____ of the other just when its antecedent is the negated consequent of the other, and vice-versa.

a. Control chart
b. Contrapositive
c. Continuous signal
d. Contour map

72. A _____ is a structured activity, usually undertaken for enjoyment and sometimes also used as an educational tool. _____s are distinct from work, which is usually carried out for remuneration, and from art, which is more concerned with the expression of ideas. However, the distinction is not clear-cut, and many _____s are also considered to be work (such as professional players of spectator sports/_____s) or art (such as jigsaw puzzles or _____s involving an artistic layout such as Mah-jongg solitaire.)

a. 2-3 heap
b. Game
c. 1-center problem
d. 120-cell

Chapter 2. SETS AND COUNTING

1. _____ is the branch of mathematics that studies sets, which are collections of objects. Although any type of objects can be collected into a set, _____ is applied most often to objects that are relevant to mathematics.

The modern study of _____ was initiated by Cantor and Dedekind in the 1870s.

- a. Logical conjunction
- b. Consistent
- c. Logical value
- d. Set theory

2. The word _____ has many distinct meanings in different fields of knowledge, depending on their methodologies and the context of discussion. Broadly speaking we can say that a _____ is some kind of belief or claim that (supposedly) explains, asserts, or consolidates some class of claims. Additionally, in contrast with a theorem the statement of the _____ is generally accepted only in some tentative fashion as opposed to regarding it as having been conclusively established.
- a. Defined
- b. Per mil
- c. Transport of structure
- d. Theory

3. In mathematics, _____ are generalized numbers used to measure the cardinality of sets. For finite sets, the cardinality is given by a natural number, which is simply the number of elements in the set. There are also transfinite _____ that describe the sizes of infinite sets.
- a. Cardinality of the continuum
- b. Suslin cardinal
- c. Strong partition cardinal
- d. Cardinal numbers

4. In mathematics, an _____ or member of a set is any one of the distinct objects that make up that set.

Writing A = {1,2,3,4}, means that the _____s of the set A are the numbers 1, 2, 3 and 4. Groups of _____s of A, for example {1,2}, are subsets of A.

- a. Universal code
- b. Order
- c. Ideal
- d. Element

5. _____ or set diagrams are diagrams that show all hypothetically possible logical relations between a finite collection of sets. _____ were invented around 1880 by John Venn. They are used in many fields, including set theory, probability, logic, statistics, and computer science.
- a. 2-3 heap
- b. 120-cell
- c. 1-center problem
- d. Venn diagrams

6. In mathematics, the term _____ is used to specify that a certain concept or object (a function, a property, a relation, etc.) is defined in a mathematical or logical way using a set of base axioms in an entirely unambiguous way and satisfies the properties it is required to satisfy. Usually definitions are stated unambiguously, and it is clear they satisfy the required properties.
- a. Defined
- b. Handwaving
- c. Quotition
- d. Well-defined

7. In mathematics, _____ and undefined are used to explain whether or not expressions have meaningful, sensible, and unambiguous values. Not all branches of mathematics come to the same conclusion.

The following expressions are undefined in all contexts, but remarks in the analysis section may apply.

Chapter 2. SETS AND COUNTING

    a. LHS   b. Defined
    c. Toy model   d. Plugging in

8. A _____ is a 2D geometric symbolic representation of information according to some visualization technique. Sometimes, the technique uses a 3D visualization which is then projected onto the 2D surface. The word graph is sometimes used as a synonym for _____.

    a. 120-cell   b. Diagram
    c. 2-3 heap   d. 1-center problem

9. In mathematics, and more specifically set theory, the _____ is the unique set having no members. Some axiomatic set theories assure that the _____ exists by including an axiom of _____; in other theories, its existence can be deduced. Many possible properties of sets are trivially true for the _____.

    a. A Mathematical Theory of Communication   b. Empty function
    c. Inverse function   d. Empty set

10. In mathematics, especially in set theory, a set A is a _____ of a set B if A is 'contained' inside B. Notice that A and B may coincide. The relationship of one set being a _____ of another is called inclusion.

    a. Subset   b. Set of all sets
    c. Cartesian product   d. Horizontal line test

11. A _____ is a software program that facilitates symbolic mathematics. The core functionality of a CAS is manipulation of mathematical expressions in symbolic form.

Chapter 2. SETS AND COUNTING

The symbolic manipulations supported typically include

- simplification to the smallest possible expression or some standard form, including automatic simplification with assumptions and simplification with constraints
- substitution of symbolic, functors or numeric values for expressions
- change of form of expressions: expanding products and powers, partial and full factorization, rewriting as partial fractions, constraint satisfaction, rewriting trigonometric functions as exponentials, etc.
- partial and total differentiation
- symbolic constrained and unconstrained global optimization
- solution of linear and some non-linear equations over various domains
- solution of some differential and difference equations
- taking some limits
- some indefinite and definite integration, including multidimensional integrals
- integral transforms
- arbitrary-precision numeric operations
- Series operations such as expansion, summation and products
- matrix operations including products, inverses, etc.
- display of mathematical expressions in two-dimensional mathematical form, often using typesetting systems similar to TeX
- add-ons for use in applied mathematics such as physics packages for physical computation
- plotting graphs and parametric plots of functions in two and three dimensions, and animating them
- APIs for linking it on an external program such as a database, or using in a programming language to use the _____
- drawing charts and diagrams
- string manipulation such as matching and searching
- statistical computation
- Theorem proving and verification
- graphic production and editing such as CGI and signal processing as image processing
- sound synthesis

Many also include a programming language, allowing users to implement their own algorithms.

Some _____s focus on a specific area of application; these are typically developed in academia and are free.

a. 2-3 heap
c. Computer algebra system

b. 1-center problem
d. 120-cell

12. In mathematics, the _____ of two sets A and B is the set that contains all elements of A that also belong to B, but no other elements.

For explanation of the symbols used in this article, refer to the table of mathematical symbols.

The _____ of A and B

The _____ of A and B is written 'A ∩ B'. Formally:

> x is an element of A ∩ B if and only if
> - x is an element of A and
> - x is an element of B.
>
> For example:
> - The _____ of the sets {1, 2, 3} and {2, 3, 4} is {2, 3}.
> - The number 9 is not in the _____ of the set of prime numbers {2, 3, 5, 7, 11, …} and the set of odd numbers {1, 3, 5, 7, 9, 11, …}.

If the _____ of two sets A and B is empty, that is they have no elements in common, then they are said to be disjoint, denoted: A ∩ B = Ø. For example the sets {1, 2} and {3, 4} are disjoint, written {1, 2} ∩ {3, 4} = Ø.

a. Erlang
b. Order
c. Advice
d. Intersection

13. In simple terms, two events are _____ if they cannot occur at the same time.

In logic, two _____ propositions are propositions that logically cannot both be true. To say that more than two propositions are _____ may, depending on context mean that no two of them can both be true, or only that they cannot all be true.

a. Philosophy
b. Mutually exclusive
c. Philosophy of mathematics
d. Determinism

14. In set theory, the term _____ refers to a set operation used in the convergence of set elements to form a resultant set containing the elements of both sets. As a simple example, a _____ of two disjoint sets, which do not have elements in common results in a set containing all elements from both sets. A Venn diagram representing the _____ of sets A and B.

a. UES
b. Event
c. Introduction
d. Union

15. In mathematics and in the sciences, a _____ (plural: _____e, formulæ or _____s) is a concise way of expressing information symbolically (as in a mathematical or chemical _____), or a general relationship between quantities. One of many famous _____e is Albert Einstein's $E = mc^2$ (see special relativity

In mathematics, a _____ is a key to solve an equation with variables. For example, the problem of determining the volume of a sphere is one that requires a significant amount of integral calculus to solve.

a. Formula
b. 2-3 heap
c. 120-cell
d. 1-center problem

Chapter 2. SETS AND COUNTING

16. In discrete mathematics and predominantly in set theory, a _____ is a concept used in comparisons of sets to refer to the unique values of one set in relation to another. The terms 'absolute' and 'relative' _____ refer to more specific applications of the concept, with universal _____s referring to elements unique to the universal set and the latter referring to the unique elements of one set in relation to another. In this image, the universal set is represented by the border of the image, and the set A as a disc.
   a. Derivative algebra
   b. Huge
   c. Complement
   d. Kernel

17. The word _____ denotes information gained by means of observation, experience as opposed to theoretical. A central concept in science and the scientific method is that all evidence must be _____ that is, dependent on evidence or consequences that are observable by the senses. It is usually differentiated from the philosophic usage of empiricism by the use of the adjective '_____' or the adverb 'empirically.' '_____' as an adjective or adverb is used in conjunction with both the natural and social sciences, and refers to the use of working hypotheses that are testable using observation or experiment.
   a. A posteriori
   b. Empirical
   c. A Mathematical Theory of Communication
   d. A chemical equation

18. _____ was a German polymath who wrote primarily in Latin and French.

He occupies an equally grand place in both the history of philosophy and the history of mathematics. He invented infinitesimal calculus independently of Newton, and his notation is the one in general use since then.

   a. Harry Hinsley
   b. Raymond Merrill Smullyan
   c. Michel Rolle
   d. Gottfried Wilhelm Leibniz

19. _____ is the study of the principles of valid demonstration and inference. _____ is a branch of philosophy, a part of the classical trivium of grammar, _____, and rhetoric. of λογικῐ́ες, 'possessed of reason, intellectual, dialectical, argumentative', from λῐ́Œγος logos, 'word, thought, idea, argument, account, reason, or principle'.
   a. Boolean function
   b. Satisfiability
   c. Logic
   d. Counterpart theory

20. _____ refers to depicting depth in 3D models or illustrations by varying levels of darkness. Example of _____.

_____ is a process used in drawing for depicting levels of darkness on paper by applying media more densely or with a darker shade for darker areas, and less densely or with a lighter shade for lighter areas. There are various techniques of _____ including cross hatching where perpendicular lines of varying closeness are drawn in a grid pattern to shade an area.

   a. Pixel shader
   b. Constructive solid geometry
   c. Radiosity
   d. Shading

21. In logic and mathematics, _____ is a logical operator connecting two statements to assert, p if and only if q where p is a hypothesis and q is a conclusion. The operator is denoted using a doubleheaded arrow '↔', an equality sign '=', an equivalence sign '≡', or EQV. It is logically equivalent to ∧, or the XNOR boolean operator.

a. Consistent
b. Logical biconditional
c. Conflation
d. Necessary and sufficient

22. In mathematics, and in particular in abstract algebra, distributivity is a property of binary operations that generalises the _____ law from elementary algebra.
   a. Closure with a twist
   b. Permutation
   c. General linear group
   d. Distributive

23. _____ IPA: [pjɛʁ ɛ dɛ™fɛʁ 'ma] (17 August 1601 or 1607/8 - 12 January 1665) was a French lawyer at the Parlement of Toulouse, France, and a mathematician who is given credit for early developments that led to modern calculus. In particular, he is recognized for his discovery of an original method of finding the greatest and the smallest ordinates of curved lines, which is analogous to that of the then unknown differential calculus, as well as his research into the theory of numbers. He also made notable contributions to analytic geometry, probability, and optics.
   a. Felix Hausdorff
   b. Philip J. Davis
   c. Nikita Borisov
   d. Pierre de Fermat

24. _____ is a branch of pure mathematics concerning the study of discrete objects. It is related to many other areas of mathematics, such as algebra, probability theory, ergodic theory and geometry, as well as to applied subjects in computer science and statistical physics. Aspects of _____ include 'counting' the objects satisfying certain criteria, deciding when the criteria can be met, and constructing and analyzing objects meeting the criteria, finding 'largest', 'smallest', or 'optimal' objects, and finding algebraic structures these objects may have.
   a. Factorial
   b. Combinatorics
   c. Combinatorial species
   d. Restricted sumset

25. In combinatorial mathematics, a _____ is an un-ordered collection of distinct elements, usually of a prescribed size and taken from a given set. Given such a set S, a _____ of elements of S is just a subset of S, where as always forsets the order of the elements is not taken into account. Also, as always forsets, no elements can be repeated more than once in a _____; this is often referred to as a 'collection without repetition'.
   a. Fill-in
   b. Heawood number
   c. Sparsity
   d. Combination

26. In several fields of mathematics the term _____ is used with different but closely related meanings. They all relate to the notion of mapping the elements of a set to other elements of the same set, i.e., exchanging elements of a set.

The general concept of _____ can be defined more formally in different contexts:

In combinatorics, a _____ is usually understood to be a sequence containing each element from a finite set once, and only once.

   a. Linearly independent
   b. Cyclic permutation
   c. Tensor product
   d. Permutation

27. In set theory, a _____ is a partially ordered set such that for each t ∈ T, the set {s ∈ T : s < t} is well-ordered by the relation <. For each t ∈ T, the order type of {s ∈ T : s < t} is called the height of t. The height of T itself is the least ordinal greater than the height of each element of T.

Chapter 2. SETS AND COUNTING

a. Transitive reduction
b. Definable numbers
c. Tree
d. Set-theoretic topology

28. In cryptography, _____ is a pseudorandom number generator and a stream cipher designed by Robert Jenkins to be cryptographically secure. The name is an acronym for Indirection, Shift, Accumulate, Add, and Count.

The _____ algorithm has similarities with RC4.

a. Imputation
b. Order
c. Introduction
d. Isaac

29. The _____ (symbol: N) is the SI derived unit of force, named after Isaac _____ in recognition of his work on classical mechanics.

The _____ is the unit of force derived in the SI system; it is equal to the amount of force required to accelerate a mass of one kilogram at a rate of one meter per second per second. Algebraically:

$$1 \text{ N} = 1 \ \frac{\text{kg} \cdot \text{m}}{\text{s}^2}.$$

- 1 N is the force of Earth's gravity on an object with a mass of about 102 g ($1/_{9.8}$ kg) (such as a small apple.)
- On Earth's surface, a mass of 1 kg exerts a force of approximately 9.80665 N [down] (or 1 kgf.) The approximation of 1 kg corresponding to 10 N is sometimes used as a rule of thumb in everyday life and in engineering.
- The force of Earth's gravity on a human being with a mass of 70 kg is approximately 687 N.
- The dot product of force and distance is mechanical work. Thus, in SI units, a force of 1 N exerted over a distance of 1 m is 1 NÂ·m of work. The Work-Energy Theorem states that the work done on a body is equal to the change in energy of the body. 1 NÂ·m = 1 J (joule), the SI unit of energy.
- It is common to see forces expressed in kilonewtons or kN, where 1 kN = 1 000 N.

a. 1-center problem
b. 2-3 heap
c. 120-cell
d. Newton

30. In mathematics, the _____ is an approach to finding a particular solution to certain inhomogeneous ordinary differential equations and recurrence relations. It is closely related to the annihilator method, but instead of using a particular kind of differential operator in order to find the best possible form of the particular solution, a 'guess' is made as to the appropriate form, which is then tested by differentiating the resulting equation. In this sense, the _____ is less formal but more intuitive than the annihilator method.

a. Linear differential equation
b. Phase line
c. Differential algebraic equations
d. Method of undetermined coefficients

Chapter 2. SETS AND COUNTING

31. In trigonometry, the _____ is a function defined as tan x = $\sin x / \cos x$. The function is so-named because it can be defined as the length of a certain segment of a _____ (in the geometric sense) to the unit circle. In plane geometry, a line is _____ to a curve, at some point, if both line and curve pass through the point with the same direction.

   a. Hopf conjectures
   b. Conformal geometry
   c. Projective connection
   d. Tangent

32. In geometry, the _____ to a curve at a given point is the straight line that 'just touches' the curve at that point. As it passes through the point of tangency, the _____ is 'going in the same direction' as the curve, and in this sense it is the best straight-line approximation to the curve at that point. The same definition applies to space curves and curves in n-dimensional Euclidean space.

   a. Darboux frame
   b. Chern-Weil theory
   c. Four-vertex theorem
   d. Tangent line

33. In mathematics, the _____ of a non-negative integer n, denoted by n!, is the product of all positive integers less than or equal to n. For example,

$$5! = 1 \times 2 \times 3 \times 4 \times 5 = 120$$

and

$$6! = 1 \times 2 \times 3 \times 4 \times 5 \times 6 = 720$$

The notation n! was introduced by Christian Kramp in 1808.

The _____ function is formally defined by

$$n! = \prod_{k=1}^{n} k \qquad \forall n \in \mathbb{N}.$$

The above definition incorporates the instance

$$0! = 1$$

as an instance of the fact that the product of no numbers at all is 1.

   a. Plane partition
   b. Symbolic combinatorics
   c. Partition of a set
   d. Factorial

34. _____ is a quantity expressing the two-dimensional size of a defined part of a surface, typically a region bounded by a closed curve. The term surface _____ refers to the total _____ of the exposed surface of a 3-dimensional solid, such as the sum of the _____ s of the exposed sides of a polyhedron. _____ is an important invariant in the differential geometry of surfaces.

Chapter 2. SETS AND COUNTING

a. A posteriori
b. Area
c. A Mathematical Theory of Communication
d. A chemical equation

35. A _____ is one of the basic shapes of geometry: a polygon with three corners or vertices and three sides or edges which are line segments. A _____ with vertices A, B, and C is denoted ABC.

In Euclidean geometry any three non-collinear points determine a unique _____ and a unique plane.

a. 1-center problem
b. Fuhrmann circle
c. Triangle
d. Kepler triangle

36. In the study of metric spaces in mathematics, there are various notions of two metrics on the same underlying space being 'the same', or _____.

In the following, M will denote a non-empty set and d_1 and d_2 will denote two metrics on M.

The two metrics d_1 and d_2 are said to be topologically _____ if they generate the same topology on M.

a. A chemical equation
b. A posteriori
c. Equivalent
d. A Mathematical Theory of Communication

37. A _____ is the result of applying a function to a set of data.

More formally, statistical theory defines a _____ as a function of a sample where the function itself is independent of the sample's distribution: the term is used both for the function and for the value of the function on a given sample.

A _____ is distinct from an unknown statistical parameter, which is not computable from a sample.

a. Parameter space
b. Spatial dependence
c. Statistic
d. Loss function

38. _____ is a mathematical science pertaining to the collection, analysis, interpretation or explanation, and presentation of data. It also provides tools for prediction and forecasting based on data. It is applicable to a wide variety of academic disciplines, from the natural and social sciences to the humanities, government and business.

a. Probability distribution
b. Statistics
c. Regression toward the mean
d. Percentile rank

39. In mathematics, a _____ is a set with the same cardinality as some subset of the set of natural numbers. The term was originated by Georg Cantor; it stems from the fact that the natural numbers are often called counting numbers. A set that is not countable is called uncountable.

a. Cofinite
b. Countable Set
c. Dedekind-infinite
d. Transfinite numbers

Chapter 2. SETS AND COUNTING

40. In mathematics, the _____ of a set is a measure of the 'number of elements of the set'. For example, the set A = {1, 2, 3} contains 3 elements, and therefore A has a _____ of 3. There are two approaches to _____ - one which compares sets directly using bijections and injections, and another which uses cardinal numbers.
   a. Cardinality
   b. 120-cell
   c. 2-3 heap
   d. 1-center problem

41. _____ Galilei (15 February 1564 - 8 January 1642) was a Tuscan physicist, mathematician, astronomer, and philosopher who played a major role in the Scientific Revolution. His achievements include improvements to the telescope and consequent astronomical observations, and support for Copernicanism. _____ has been called the 'father of modern observational astronomy', the 'father of modern physics', the 'father of science', and 'the Father of Modern Science.' The motion of uniformly accelerated objects, taught in nearly all high school and introductory college physics courses, was studied by _____ as the subject of kinematics.
   a. Francesco Severi
   b. David Naccache
   c. Jan Kowalewski
   d. Galileo

42. In mathematics, an _____ is an infinite set which is too big to be countable. The uncountability of a set is closely related to its cardinal number: a set is uncountable if its cardinal number is larger than that of the natural numbers. The related term nondenumerable set is used by some authors as a synonym for '_____' while other authors define a set to be nondenumerable if it is not an infinite countable set.
   a. A chemical equation
   b. A Mathematical Theory of Communication
   c. A posteriori
   d. Uncountable set

43. In mathematics, the word _____ has at least two distinct meanings, outlined in the sections below. For other uses see _____.

The term the _____ sometimes denotes the real line.

   a. Coordinate rotations and reflections
   b. Barrelled spaces
   c. Continuum
   d. Christofides heuristics algorithm

44. In mathematics, the _____ is a hypothesis, advanced by Georg Cantor, about the possible sizes of infinite sets. Cantor introduced the concept of cardinality to compare the sizes of infinite sets, and he gave two proofs that the cardinality of the set of integers is strictly smaller than that of the set of real numbers. His proofs, however, give no indication of the extent to which the cardinality of the natural numbers is less than that of the real numbers.
   a. Blotto game
   b. Continuum Hypothesis
   c. Compact groups
   d. Closed under some operation

45. In mathematics, the _____s may be described informally in several different ways. The _____s include both rational numbers, such as 42 and −23/129, and irrational numbers, such as pi and the square root of two; or, a _____ can be given by an infinite decimal representation, such as 2.4871773339...., where the digits continue in some way; or, the _____s may be thought of as points on an infinitely long number line.

These descriptions of the _____s, while intuitively accessible, are not sufficiently rigorous for the purposes of pure mathematics.

a. Tally marks
b. Minkowski distance
c. Pre-algebra
d. Real number

46. In mathematics, a _____ is a set of numbers,, together with one or more operations, such as addition or multiplication.

Examples of _____s include: natural numbers, integers, rational numbers, algebraic numbers, real numbers, complex numbers, p-adic numbers, surreal numbers, and hyperreal numbers.

a. Slope
b. Number system
c. Tally marks
d. Number line

Chapter 3. PROBABILITY

1. _____ is the likelihood or chance that something is the case or will happen. Theoretical _____ is used extensively in areas such as statistics, mathematics, science and philosophy to draw conclusions about the likelihood of potential events and the underlying mechanics of complex systems.

The word _____ does not have a consistent direct definition.

   a. Discrete random variable
   b. Statistical significance
   c. Standardized moment
   d. Probability

2. _____ IPA: [pjɛʁ ɛ dɛ™fɛʁ 'ma] (17 August 1601 or 1607/8 - 12 January 1665) was a French lawyer at the Parlement of Toulouse, France, and a mathematician who is given credit for early developments that led to modern calculus. In particular, he is recognized for his discovery of an original method of finding the greatest and the smallest ordinates of curved lines, which is analogous to that of the then unknown differential calculus, as well as his research into the theory of numbers. He also made notable contributions to analytic geometry, probability, and optics.

   a. Pierre de Fermat
   b. Felix Hausdorff
   c. Nikita Borisov
   d. Philip J. Davis

3. A _____ is a structured activity, usually undertaken for enjoyment and sometimes also used as an educational tool. _____s are distinct from work, which is usually carried out for remuneration, and from art, which is more concerned with the expression of ideas. However, the distinction is not clear-cut, and many _____s are also considered to be work (such as professional players of spectator sports/_____s) or art (such as jigsaw puzzles or _____s involving an artistic layout such as Mah-jongg solitaire.)

   a. 2-3 heap
   b. Game
   c. 120-cell
   d. 1-center problem

4. _____ is a casino and gambling game named after the French word meaning 'small wheel'. In the game, players may choose to place bets on either a number, a range of numbers, the color red or black, or whether the number is odd or even. To determine the winning number and color, a croupier spins a wheel in one direction, then spins a ball in the opposite direction around a tilted circular track running around the circumference of the wheel.

   a. 1-center problem
   b. 120-cell
   c. 2-3 heap
   d. Roulette

5. _____ are small polyhedral objects, usually cubic, used for generating random numbers or other symbols. This makes _____ suitable as gambling devices, especially for craps or sic bo, or for use in non-gambling tabletop games.

A traditional die is a cube, marked on each of its six faces with a different number of circular patches or pits called pips.

   a. 2-3 heap
   b. 1-center problem
   c. Dice
   d. 120-cell

6. The term _____ refers to the central sense organ complex, for those animals that have one, normally on the ventral surface of the head and can depending on the definition in the human case, include the hair, forehead, eyebrow, eyes, nose, ears, cheeks, mouth, lips, philtrum, teeth, skin, and chin. The _____ has uses of expression, appearance, and identity amongst others. It also has different senses like smelling, tasting, hearing, and seeing.

Chapter 3. PROBABILITY

Caricatures often exaggerate facial features to make a _____ more easily recognized in association with a pronounced portion of the _____ of the individual in question--for example, a caricature of Osama bin Laden might focus on his facial hair and nose; a caricature of George W. Bush might enlarge his ears to the size of an elephant¢s; a caricature of Jay Leno may pronounce his head and chin; and a caricature of Mick Jagger might enlarge his lips.

a. 2-3 heap
c. 1-center problem
b. Face
d. 120-cell

7. In probability theory, an _____ is a set of outcomes to which a probability is assigned. Typically, when the sample space is finite, any subset of the sample space is an _____. However, this approach does not work well in cases where the sample space is infinite, most notably when the outcome is a real number.

a. Event
c. Equaliser
b. Audio compression
d. Information set

8. In scientific inquiry, an _____ is a method of investigating particular types of research questions or solving particular types of problems. The _____ is a cornerstone in the empirical approach to acquiring deeper knowledge about the world and is used in both natural sciences as well as in social sciences. An _____ is defined, in science, as a method of investigating less known fields, solving practical problems and proving theoretical assumptions.

a. A Mathematical Theory of Communication
c. Experiment
b. A chemical equation
d. A posteriori

9. In game theory, an _____ is a set of moves or strategies taken by the players, or their payoffs resulting from the actions or strategies taken by all players. The two are complementary in that given knowledge of the set of strategies of all players, the final state of the game is known, as are any relevant payoffs. In a game where chance or a random event is involved, the _____ is not known from only the set of strategies, but is only realized when the random even are realized.

a. Autonomous system
c. Equaliser
b. Algebraic
d. Outcome

10. In statistics, a _____ is a subset of a population. Typically, the population is very large, making a census or a complete enumeration of all the values in the population impractical or impossible. The _____ represents a subset of manageable size.

a. Sample
c. Boussinesq approximation
b. Dispersion
d. Duality

11. In probability theory, the _____ or universal _____, often denoted S, Ω of an experiment or random trial is the set of all possible outcomes. For example, if the experiment is tossing a coin, the _____ is the set {head, tail}. For tossing a single six-sided die, the _____ is {1, 2, 3, 4, 5, 6}.

a. Marginal distribution
c. Markov chain
b. Martingale central limit theorem
d. Sample space

12. In probability theory and statistics the _____ in favour of an event or a proposition are the quantity p /, where p is the probability of the event or proposition. The _____ against the same event are / p. For example, if you chose a random day of the week, then the _____ that you would choose a Sunday would be 1/6, not 1/7.

Chapter 3. PROBABILITY

a. Estimation of covariance matrices
b. Event
c. Anscombe transform
d. Odds

13. A _____ is one of the basic shapes of geometry: a polygon with three corners or vertices and three sides or edges which are line segments. A _____ with vertices A, B, and C is denoted ABC.

In Euclidean geometry any three non-collinear points determine a unique _____ and a unique plane.

a. 1-center problem
b. Kepler triangle
c. Fuhrmann circle
d. Triangle

14. _____ is a branch of mathematics that deals with triangles, particularly those plane triangles in which one angle has 90 degrees. _____ deals with relationships between the sides and the angles of triangles and with the trigonometric functions, which describe those relationships.

_____ has applications in both pure mathematics and in applied mathematics, where it is essential in many branches of science and technology.

a. Law of sines
b. Sine
c. Trigonometric functions
d. Trigonometry

15. The _____ is a theorem in probability that describes the long-term stability of the mean of a random variable. Given a random variable with a finite expected value, if its values are repeatedly sampled, as the number of these observations increases, their mean will tend to approach and stay close to the expected value.

The LLN can easily be illustrated using the rolls of a die.

a. Point process
b. Graphical model
c. Random field
d. Law of large numbers

16. In statistics the _____ of an event i is the number n_i of times the event occurred in the experiment or the study. These frequencies are often graphically represented in histograms.

We speak of absolute frequencies, when the counts n_i themselves are given and of

$$f_i = \frac{n_i}{N} = \frac{n_i}{\sum_i n_i}$$

Taking the f_i for all i and tabulating or plotting them leads to a _____ distribution.

a. Subharmonic
b. Frequency
c. Digital room correction
d. Robinson-Dadson curves

Chapter 3. PROBABILITY

17. In mathematics and physics, there are a _____ number of topics named in honor of Leonhard Euler. As well, many of these topics include their own unique function, equation, formula, identity, number, or other mathematical entity. Unfortunately however, many of these entities have been given simple names like Euler's function, Euler's equation, and Euler's formula, which are further confused by variations of the 'Euler'-prefix Overall though, Euler's work touched upon so many fields that he is often the earliest written reference on a given matter.
   a. List of integrals of logarithmic functions
   b. List of mathematical knots and links
   c. Large
   d. List of trigonometry topics

18. The _____ is a diagram that is used to predict the outcome of a particular cross or breeding experiment. It is named after Reginald C. Punnett, who devised the approach, and is used by biologists to determine the probability of an offspring having a particular genotype.
   a. Genetics
   b. Punnett square
   c. Hardy-Weinberg principle
   d. Significance analysis of microarrays

19. _____ , a discipline of biology, is the science of heredity and variation in living organisms. The fact that living things inherit traits from their parents has been used since prehistoric times to improve crop plants and animals through selective breeding. However, the modern science of _____, which seeks to understand the process of inheritance, only began with the work of Gregor Mendel in the mid-nineteenth century.
   a. Polytomy
   b. Fitness landscapes
   c. Genetics
   d. Hardy-Weinberg principle

20. In set theory, a _____ is a partially ordered set such that for each $t \in T$, the set $\{s \in T : s < t\}$ is well-ordered by the relation <. For each $t \in T$, the order type of $\{s \in T : s < t\}$ is called the height of t. The height of T itself is the least ordinal greater than the height of each element of T.
   a. Set-theoretic topology
   b. Definable numbers
   c. Transitive reduction
   d. Tree

21. A _____ is a 2D geometric symbolic representation of information according to some visualization technique. Sometimes, the technique uses a 3D visualization which is then projected onto the 2D surface. The word graph is sometimes used as a synonym for _____.
   a. 1-center problem
   b. 2-3 heap
   c. 120-cell
   d. Diagram

22. A _____ is an algebraic equation in which each term is either a constant or the product of a constant and a single variable. _____s can have one, two, three or more variables.

   _____s occur with great regularity in applied mathematics.

   a. Difference of two squares
   b. Linear equation
   c. Quadratic equation
   d. Quartic equation

23. In mathematics, a _____ is a set that is negligible in some sense. For different applications, the meaning of 'negligible' varies. In measure theory, any set of measure 0 is called a _____.
   a. Prevalence and shyness
   b. Null set
   c. Borel-Cantelli lemma
   d. Radonifying function

32 **Chapter 3. PROBABILITY**

24. In simple terms, two events are _____ if they cannot occur at the same time.

In logic, two _____ propositions are propositions that logically cannot both be true. To say that more than two propositions are _____ may, depending on context mean that no two of them can both be true, or only that they cannot all be true.

   a. Philosophy
   b. Philosophy of mathematics
   c. Determinism
   d. Mutually exclusive

25. _____ or set diagrams are diagrams that show all hypothetically possible logical relations between a finite collection of sets. _____ were invented around 1880 by John Venn. They are used in many fields, including set theory, probability, logic, statistics, and computer science.
   a. 2-3 heap
   b. 120-cell
   c. 1-center problem
   d. Venn diagrams

26. A _____ is a software program that facilitates symbolic mathematics. The core functionality of a CAS is manipulation of mathematical expressions in symbolic form.

Chapter 3. PROBABILITY

The symbolic manipulations supported typically include

- simplification to the smallest possible expression or some standard form, including automatic simplification with assumptions and simplification with constraints
- substitution of symbolic, functors or numeric values for expressions
- change of form of expressions: expanding products and powers, partial and full factorization, rewriting as partial fractions, constraint satisfaction, rewriting trigonometric functions as exponentials, etc.
- partial and total differentiation
- symbolic constrained and unconstrained global optimization
- solution of linear and some non-linear equations over various domains
- solution of some differential and difference equations
- taking some limits
- some indefinite and definite integration, including multidimensional integrals
- integral transforms
- arbitrary-precision numeric operations
- Series operations such as expansion, summation and products
- matrix operations including products, inverses, etc.
- display of mathematical expressions in two-dimensional mathematical form, often using typesetting systems similar to TeX
- add-ons for use in applied mathematics such as physics packages for physical computation
- plotting graphs and parametric plots of functions in two and three dimensions, and animating them
- APIs for linking it on an external program such as a database, or using in a programming language to use the _____
- drawing charts and diagrams
- string manipulation such as matching and searching
- statistical computation
- Theorem proving and verification
- graphic production and editing such as CGI and signal processing as image processing
- sound synthesis

Many also include a programming language, allowing users to implement their own algorithms.

Some _____s focus on a specific area of application; these are typically developed in academia and are free.

a. Computer algebra system
c. 1-center problem
b. 120-cell
d. 2-3 heap

27. A _____ typically refers to a class of handheld calculators that are capable of plotting graphs, solving simultaneous equations, and performing numerous other tasks with variables. Most popular _____s are also programmable, allowing the user to create customized programs, typically for scientific/engineering and education applications. Due to their large displays intended for graphing, they can also accommodate several lines of text and calculations at a time.

34   *Chapter 3. PROBABILITY*

a. Bump mapping
b. Graphing calculator
c. Support vector machines
d. Genus

28. _____ or amortisation is the process of decreasing an amount over a period of time. The word comes from Middle English amortisen to kill, alienate in mortmain, from Anglo-French amorteser, alteration of amortir, from Vulgar Latin admortire to kill, from Latin ad- + mort-, mors death. Particular instances of the term include:

- _____, the allocation of a lump sum amount to different time periods, particularly for loans and other forms of finance, including related interest or other finance charges.
    - _____ schedule, a table detailing each periodic payment on a loan, as generated by an _____ calculator.
    - Negative _____, an _____ schedule where the loan amount actually increases through not paying the full interest
- Amortized analysis, analyzing the execution cost of algorithms over a sequence of operations.
- _____ of capital expenditures of certain assets under accounting rules, particularly intangible assets, in a manner analogous to depreciation.
- _____

_____ is also used in the context of zoning regulations and describes the time in which a property owner has to relocate when the property's use constitutes a preexisting nonconforming use under zoning regulations.

- Depreciation

a. ISAAC
b. Identity
c. Origin
d. Amortization

29. An _____ is a table detailing each periodic payment on a amortizing loan, as generated by an amortization calculator.

While a portion of every payment is applied towards both the interest and the principal balance of the loan, the exact amount applied to principal each time varies. An _____ reveals the specific monetary amount put towards interest, as well as the specific put towards the Principal balance, with each payment.

a. Amortization schedule
b. A chemical equation
c. Accounts receivable
d. A Mathematical Theory of Communication

30. A _____ is a device for performing mathematical calculations, distinguished from a computer by having a limited problem solving ability and an interface optimized for interactive calculation rather than programming. _____s can be hardware or software, and mechanical or electronic, and are often built into devices such as PDAs or mobile phones.

Modern electronic _____s are generally small, digital, and usually inexpensive.

a. 2-3 heap
b. 1-center problem
c. Calculator
d. 120-cell

Chapter 3. PROBABILITY

31. _____ is a branch of pure mathematics concerning the study of discrete objects. It is related to many other areas of mathematics, such as algebra, probability theory, ergodic theory and geometry, as well as to applied subjects in computer science and statistical physics. Aspects of _____ include 'counting' the objects satisfying certain criteria, deciding when the criteria can be met, and constructing and analyzing objects meeting the criteria, finding 'largest', 'smallest', or 'optimal' objects, and finding algebraic structures these objects may have.

- a. Factorial
- b. Combinatorial species
- c. Restricted sumset
- d. Combinatorics

32. _____ is the wagering of money or something of material value on an event with an uncertain outcome with the primary intent of winning additional money and/or material goods. Typically, the outcome of the wager is evident within a short period.

The term gaming in this context typically refers to instances in which the activity has been specifically permitted by law.

- a. 2-3 heap
- b. 1-center problem
- c. 120-cell
- d. Gambling

33. In probability theory and statistics, the _____ of a random variable is the integral of the random variable with respect to its probability measure. For discrete random variables this is equivalent to the probability-weighted sum of the possible values, and for continuous random variables with a density function it is the probability density -weighted integral of the possible values.

The _____ may be intuitively understood by the law of large numbers: The _____, when it exists, is almost surely the limit of the sample mean as sample size grows to infinity.

- a. Infinitely divisible distribution
- b. Illustration
- c. Event
- d. Expected value

34. In mathematics, _____ and undefined are used to explain whether or not expressions have meaningful, sensible, and unambiguous values. Not all branches of mathematics come to the same conclusion.

The following expressions are undefined in all contexts, but remarks in the analysis section may apply.

- a. Toy model
- b. LHS
- c. Defined
- d. Plugging in

35. _____ in mathematics and statistics is concerned with identifying the values, uncertainties and other issues relevant in a given decision and the resulting optimal decision.

Most of _____ is normative or prescriptive. The practical application of this prescriptive approach is called decision analysis, and aimed at finding tools, methodologies and software to help people make better decisions.

- a. Pignistic probability
- b. Subjective expected utility
- c. Probabilistic Prognosis
- d. Decision theory

Chapter 3. PROBABILITY

36. Originally, _____ referred to a class of betting strategies popular in 18th-century France. The simplest of these strategies was designed for a game in which the gambler wins his stake if a coin comes up heads and loses it if the coin comes up tails. The strategy had the gambler double his bet after every loss, so that the first win would recover all previous losses plus win a profit equal to the original stake.

a. Constructivism
b. Brute Force
c. Huge
d. Martingale

37. In game theory, a player's _____ in a game is a complete plan of action for whatever situation might arise; this fully determines the player's behaviour. A player's _____ will determine the action the player will take at any stage of the game, for every possible history of play up to that stage.

A _____ profile is a set of strategies for each player which fully specifies all actions in a game.

a. Sir Philip Sidney game
b. Correlated equilibrium
c. Matching pennies
d. Strategy

38. The word _____ has many distinct meanings in different fields of knowledge, depending on their methodologies and the context of discussion. Broadly speaking we can say that a _____ is some kind of belief or claim that (supposedly) explains, asserts, or consolidates some class of claims. Additionally, in contrast with a theorem the statement of the _____ is generally accepted only in some tentative fashion as opposed to regarding it as having been conclusively established.

a. Per mil
b. Defined
c. Transport of structure
d. Theory

39. _____ is the probability of some event A, given the occurrence of some other event B. _____ is written P[A | B], and is read 'the probability of A, given B'.

Joint probability is the probability of two events in conjunction. That is, it is the probability of both events together. The joint probability of A and B is written $P(A \cap B)$ or $P(A,B)$.

a. Conditional probability
b. Renewal theory
c. Quantile
d. Sample space

40. The _____ governs the differentiation of products of differentiable functions.

a. 1-center problem
b. 120-cell
c. Reciprocal Rule
d. Product rule

41. In statistics, the terms Type I error and type II error are used to describe possible errors made in a statistical decision process. In 1928, Jerzy Neyman and Egon Pearson, both eminent statisticians, discussed the problems associated with 'deciding whether or not a particular sample may be judged as likely to have been randomly drawn from a certain population': and identified 'two sources of error', namely:

null hypothesis, and
null hypothesis

In 1930, they elaborated on these two sources of error, remarking that 'in testing hypotheses two considerations must be kept in view, we must be able to reduce the chance of rejecting a true hypothesis to as low a value as desired; the test must be so devised that it will reject the hypothesis tested when it is likely to be false'

When an observer makes a Type I error in evaluating a sample against its parent population, s/he is mistakenly thinking that a statistical difference exists when in truth there is no statistical difference. For example, imagine that a pregnancy test has produced a 'positive' result; if the woman is actually not pregnant though, then we say the test produced a '_____'.

a. Mathematical statistics
b. False positive
c. Covariance
d. Chi-square test

Chapter 4. STATISTICS

1. In statistics, a _____ is a single typed measurement. Here type is used in a way compatible with datatype in computing; so that the type of measurement can specify whether the measurement results in a Boolean value from {yes, no}, an integer or real number, or some vector or array. The implication of point is therefore that the data may be plotted in a graphic display, but in many cases the data are processed numerically before that is done.
   a. Conditionality principle
   b. Statistical model
   c. Sensitivity and specificity
   d. Data point

2. _____ are used to describe the basic features of the data gathered from an experimental study in various ways. A _____ is distinguished from inductive statistics. They provide simple summaries about the sample and the measures.
   a. Null hypothesis
   b. Failure rate
   c. Biostatistics
   d. Descriptive statistics

3. In statistics the _____ of an event i is the number n_i of times the event occurred in the experiment or the study. These frequencies are often graphically represented in histograms.

   We speak of absolute frequencies, when the counts n_i themselves are given and of

   $$f_i = \frac{n_i}{N} = \frac{n_i}{\sum_i n_i}$$

   Taking the f_i for all i and tabulating or plotting them leads to a _____ distribution.

   a. Digital room correction
   b. Subharmonic
   c. Frequency
   d. Robinson-Dadson curves

4. In statistics, a _____ is a list of the values that a variable takes in a sample. It is usually a list, ordered by quantity, showing the number of times each value appears. For example, if 100 people rate a five-point Likert scale assessing their agreement with a statement on a scale on which 1 denotes strong agreement and 5 strong disagreement, the _____ of their responses might look like:

   This simple tabulation has two drawbacks.

   a. Confounding
   b. Covariance
   c. Frequency distribution
   d. Percentile

5. In statistics, a _____ is a subset of a population. Typically, the population is very large, making a census or a complete enumeration of all the values in the population impractical or impossible. The _____ represents a subset of manageable size.
   a. Duality
   b. Dispersion
   c. Sample
   d. Boussinesq approximation

6. A _____ is the result of applying a function to a set of data.

   More formally, statistical theory defines a _____ as a function of a sample where the function itself is independent of the sample's distribution: the term is used both for the function and for the value of the function on a given sample.

Chapter 4. STATISTICS

A _____ is distinct from an unknown statistical parameter, which is not computable from a sample.

    a. Spatial dependence
    b. Statistic
    c. Parameter space
    d. Loss function

7. _____ is a mathematical science pertaining to the collection, analysis, interpretation or explanation, and presentation of data. It also provides tools for prediction and forecasting based on data. It is applicable to a wide variety of academic disciplines, from the natural and social sciences to the humanities, government and business.

    a. Statistics
    b. Probability distribution
    c. Regression toward the mean
    d. Percentile rank

8. In differential geometry, a discipline within mathematics, a _____ is a subset of the tangent bundle of a manifold satisfying certain properties. _____s are used to build up notions of integrability, and specifically of a foliation of a manifold

    a. Discontinuity
    b. Constraint
    c. Coherence
    d. Distribution

9. The _____ or Dirac's delta is a mathematical construct introduced by the British theoretical physicist Paul Dirac. Informally, it is a function representing an infinitely sharp peak bounding unit area: a function that has the value zero everywhere except at x = 0 where its value is infinitely large in such a way that its total integral is 1. It is a continuous analogue of the discrete Kronecker delta.

    a. Weak derivative
    b. Dirac delta
    c. Schwartz kernel theorem
    d. Hyperfunction

10. In statistics, a _____ is a graphical display of tabulated frequencies, shown as bars. It shows what proportion of cases fall into each of several categories. A _____ differs from a bar chart in that it is the area of the bar that denotes the value, not the height as in bar charts, a crucial distinction when the categories are not of uniform width.

    a. Standardized moment
    b. First-hitting-time models
    c. Probability distribution
    d. Histogram

11. In mathematics, _____ and undefined are used to explain whether or not expressions have meaningful, sensible, and unambiguous values. Not all branches of mathematics come to the same conclusion.

The following expressions are undefined in all contexts, but remarks in the analysis section may apply.

    a. LHS
    b. Toy model
    c. Defined
    d. Plugging in

12. The _____ of a material is defined as its mass per unit volume:

$$\rho = \frac{m}{V}$$

Different materials usually have different densities, so _____ is an important concept regarding buoyancy, metal purity and packaging.

In some cases _____ is expressed as the dimensionless quantities specific gravity or relative _____, in which case it is expressed in multiples of the _____ of some other standard material, usually water or air.

In a well-known story, Archimedes was given the task of determining whether King Hiero's goldsmith was embezzling gold during the manufacture of a wreath dedicated to the gods and replacing it with another, cheaper alloy.

   a. Density
   b. 2-3 heap
   c. 1-center problem
   d. 120-cell

13. In mathematics, a _____ is a set of real numbers with the property that any number that lies between two numbers in the set is also included in the set. For example, the set of all numbers x satisfying $0 \leq x \leq 1$ is an _____ which contains 0 and 1, as well as all numbers between them. Other examples of _____s are the set of all real numbers $\mathbb{R}$, the set of all positive real numbers, and the empty set.

   a. Order
   b. Ideal
   c. Annihilator
   d. Interval

14. In set theory and its applications throughout mathematics, a _____ is a collection of sets that can be unambiguously defined by a property that all its members share. The precise definition of '_____' depends on foundational context. In work on ZF set theory, the notion of _____ is informal, whereas other set theories, such as NBG set theory, axiomatize the notion of '_____'.

   a. Class
   b. Congruent
   c. Filter
   d. Coherence

15. A _____ is a circular chart divided into sectors, illustrating relative magnitudes or frequences or percents. In a _____, the arc length of each sector, is proportional to the quantity it represents. Together, the sectors create a full disk.

   a. 120-cell
   b. 1-center problem
   c. 2-3 heap
   d. Pie chart

16. In linear algebra, _____ is a version of Gaussian elimination that puts zeros both above and below each pivot element as it goes from the top row of the given matrix to the bottom. In other words, _____ brings a matrix to reduced row echelon form, whereas Gaussian elimination takes it only as far as row echelon form. Every matrix has a reduced row echelon form, and this algorithm is guaranteed to produce it.

   a. Lax equivalence theorem
   b. Spheroidal wave functions
   c. Conservation form
   d. Gauss-Jordan elimination

17. A _____ is a device for performing mathematical calculations, distinguished from a computer by having a limited problem solving ability and an interface optimized for interactive calculation rather than programming. _____s can be hardware or software, and mechanical or electronic, and are often built into devices such as PDAs or mobile phones.

Modern electronic _____s are generally small, digital, and usually inexpensive.

   a. 120-cell
   b. 1-center problem
   c. 2-3 heap
   d. Calculator

Chapter 4. STATISTICS 41

18. A _____ typically refers to a class of handheld calculators that are capable of plotting graphs, solving simultaneous equations, and performing numerous other tasks with variables. Most popular _____s are also programmable, allowing the user to create customized programs, typically for scientific/engineering and education applications. Due to their large displays intended for graphing, they can also accommodate several lines of text and calculations at a time.

    a. Bump mapping   b. Genus
    c. Support vector machines   d. Graphing calculator

19. _____ or amortisation is the process of decreasing an amount over a period of time. The word comes from Middle English amortisen to kill, alienate in mortmain, from Anglo-French amorteser, alteration of amortir, from Vulgar Latin admortire to kill, from Latin ad- + mort-, mors death. Particular instances of the term include:

- _____, the allocation of a lump sum amount to different time periods, particularly for loans and other forms of finance, including related interest or other finance charges.
  - _____ schedule, a table detailing each periodic payment on a loan, as generated by an _____ calculator.
  - Negative _____, an _____ schedule where the loan amount actually increases through not paying the full interest
- Amortized analysis, analyzing the execution cost of algorithms over a sequence of operations.
- _____ of capital expenditures of certain assets under accounting rules, particularly intangible assets, in a manner analogous to depreciation.
- _____

_____ is also used in the context of zoning regulations and describes the time in which a property owner has to relocate when the property's use constitutes a preexisting nonconforming use under zoning regulations.

- Depreciation

    a. ISAAC   b. Identity
    c. Origin   d. Amortization

20. An _____ is a table detailing each periodic payment on a amortizing loan, as generated by an amortization calculator.

While a portion of every payment is applied towards both the interest and the principal balance of the loan, the exact amount applied to principal each time varies. An _____ reveals the specific monetary amount put towards interest, as well as the specific put towards the Principal balance, with each payment.

    a. A Mathematical Theory of Communication   b. Accounts receivable
    c. A chemical equation   d. Amortization schedule

21. In mathematics the concept of a _____ generalizes notions such as 'length', 'area', and 'volume'. Informally, given some base set, a '_____' is any consistent assignment of 'sizes' to the subsets of the base set. Depending on the application, the 'size' of a subset may be interpreted as its physical size, the amount of something that lies within the subset, or the probability that some random process will yield a result within the subset.

Chapter 4. STATISTICS

   a. Cusp
   c. Congruent
   b. Lattice
   d. Measure

22. In mathematics, an average, or _____ of a data set refers to a measure of the 'middle' or 'expected' value of the data set. There are many different descriptive statistics that can be chosen as a measurement of the _____ of the data items.

An average is a single value that is meant to typify a list of values.

   a. Central tendency
   c. Mean reciprocal rank
   b. Quartile
   d. Trimean

23. In statistics, _____ has two related meanings:

   - the arithmetic _____.
   - the expected value of a random variable, which is also called the population _____.

It is sometimes stated that the '_____' _____s average. This is incorrect if '_____' is taken in the specific sense of 'arithmetic _____' as there are different types of averages: the _____, median, and mode. For instance, average house prices almost always use the median value for the average.

For a real-valued random variable X, the _____ is the expectation of X.

   a. Probability
   c. Proportional hazards model
   b. Statistical population
   d. Mean

24. _____ is the addition of a set of numbers; the result is their sum or total. An interim or present total of a _____ process is termed the running total. The 'numbers' to be summed may be natural numbers, complex numbers, matrices, or still more complicated objects.
   a. 1-center problem
   c. 2-3 heap
   b. 120-cell
   d. Summation

25. A calculation is a deliberate process for transforming one or more inputs into one or more results, with variable change.

The term is used in a variety of senses, from the very definite arithmetical using an algorithm to the vague heuristics of _____ a strategy in a competition or _____ the chance of a successful relationship between two people.

Multiplying 7 by 8 is a simple algorithmic calculation.

   a. Calculating
   c. Mathematics Subject Classification
   b. Calculation
   d. Mathematical maturity

26. In geometry, a _____ of a triangle is a line segment joining a vertex to the midpoint of the opposing side. Every triangle has exactly three _____s; one running from each vertex to the opposite side.

Chapter 4. STATISTICS

The three _____s are concurrent at a point known as the triangle's centroid, or center of mass of the triangle.

a. Statistical significance
b. Percentile rank
c. Median
d. Correlation

27. In statistics, an _____ is an observation that is numerically distant from the rest of the data. Statistics derived from data sets that include _____s may be misleading. For example, if one is calculating the average temperature of 10 objects in a room, and most are between 20 and 25 degrees Celsius, but an oven is at 175 °C, the median of the data may be 23 °C but the mean temperature will be between 35.5 and 40 °C.

a. A Mathematical Theory of Communication
b. A chemical equation
c. A posteriori
d. Outlier

28. In mathematics, an _____, or central tendency of a data set refers to a measure of the 'middle' or 'expected' value of the data set. There are many different descriptive statistics that can be chosen as a measurement of the central tendency of the data items.

An _____ is a single value that is meant to typify a list of values.

a. A Mathematical Theory of Communication
b. A chemical equation
c. A posteriori
d. Average

29. In statistics, the _____ is the value that occurs the most frequently in a data set or a probability distribution. In some fields, notably education, sample data are often called scores, and the sample _____ is known as the modal score.

Like the statistical mean and the median, the _____ is a way of capturing important information about a random variable or a population in a single quantity.

a. Field
b. Function
c. Deltoid
d. Mode

30. In mathematics and statistics, _____ is a measure of difference for interval and ratio variables between the observed value and the mean. The sign of _____, either positive or negative, indicates whether the observation is larger than or smaller than the mean. The magnitude of the value reports how different an observation is from the mean.

a. Conchoid
b. Filter
c. Functional
d. Deviation

31. In optics, _____ is the phenomenon in which the phase velocity of a wave depends on its frequency. Media having such a property are termed dispersive media.

The most familiar example of _____ is probably a rainbow, in which _____ causes the spatial separation of a white light into components of different wavelengths.

Chapter 4. STATISTICS

a. Boussinesq approximation
b. Depth
c. Dispersion
d. Crib

32. In probability theory and statistics, the _____ of a random variable, probability distribution averaging the squared distance of its possible values from the expected value. Whereas the mean is a way to describe the location of a distribution, the _____ is a way to capture its scale or degree of being spread out. The unit of _____ is the square of the unit of the original variable.

   a. Nonlinear regression
   b. Probability distribution
   c. Kendall tau rank correlation coefficient
   d. Variance

33. In probability and statistics, the _____ is a measure of the dispersion of a collection of numbers. It can apply to a probability distribution, a random variable, a population or a data set. The _____ is usually denoted with the letter σ.

   a. Statistical population
   b. Null hypothesis
   c. Standard deviation
   d. Failure rate

34. _____ is a quantity expressing the two-dimensional size of a defined part of a surface, typically a region bounded by a closed curve. The term surface _____ refers to the total _____ of the exposed surface of a 3-dimensional solid, such as the sum of the _____s of the exposed sides of a polyhedron. _____ is an important invariant in the differential geometry of surfaces.

   a. A chemical equation
   b. A Mathematical Theory of Communication
   c. A posteriori
   d. Area

35. In mathematics and in the sciences, a _____ (plural: _____e, formulæ or _____s) is a concise way of expressing information symbolically (as in a mathematical or chemical _____), or a general relationship between quantities. One of many famous _____e is Albert Einstein's E = mc² (see special relativity

In mathematics, a _____ is a key to solve an equation with variables. For example, the problem of determining the volume of a sphere is one that requires a significant amount of integral calculus to solve.

   a. 2-3 heap
   b. Formula
   c. 1-center problem
   d. 120-cell

36. A _____ is one of the basic shapes of geometry: a polygon with three corners or vertices and three sides or edges which are line segments. A _____ with vertices A, B, and C is denoted ABC.

In Euclidean geometry any three non-collinear points determine a unique _____ and a unique plane.

   a. Fuhrmann circle
   b. 1-center problem
   c. Triangle
   d. Kepler triangle

37. In probability theory, a probability distribution is called _____ if its cumulative distribution function is _____. That is equivalent to saying that for random variables X with the distribution in question, Pr[X = a] = 0 for all real numbers a. If the distribution of X is _____ then X is called a _____ random variable.

   a. Continuous phase modulation
   b. Conull set
   c. Concatenated codes
   d. Continuous

Chapter 4. STATISTICS

38. In mathematics, the concept of a _____ tries to capture the intuitive idea of a geometrical one-dimensional and continuous object. A simple example is the circle. In everyday use of the term '_____', a straight line is not curved, but in mathematical parlance _____s include straight lines and line segments.
  a. Kappa curve
  b. Negative pedal curve
  c. Quadrifolium
  d. Curve

39. In statistics, _____ is a form of regression analysis in which the relationship between one or more independent variables and another variable, called dependent variable, is modeled by a least squares function, called _____ equation. This function is a linear combination of one or more model parameters, called regression coefficients. A _____ equation with one independent variable represents a straight line.
  a. Kurtosis
  b. Random variables
  c. Percentile rank
  d. Linear regression

40. In mathematics, specifically in combinatorial commutative algebra, a convex lattice polytope P is called _____ if it has the following property: given any positive integer n, every lattice point of the dilation nP, obtained from P by scaling its vertices by the factor n and taking the convex hull of the resulting points, can be written as the sum of exactly n lattice points in P. This property plays an important role in the theory of toric varieties, where it corresponds to projective normality of the toric variety determined by P.

The simplex in R^k with the vertices at the origin and along the unit coordinate vectors is _____.

  a. Hypercube
  b. Normal
  c. Polytetrahedron
  d. Demihypercubes

41. The _____ is an important family of continuous probability distributions, applicable in many fields. Each member of the family may be defined by two parameters, location and scale: the mean and variance respectively. The standard _____ is the _____ with a mean of zero and a variance of one.
  a. Percentile rank
  b. Coefficient of variation
  c. Null hypothesis
  d. Normal distribution

42. The _____ fallacy is an informal fallacy. It ascribes cause where none exists. The flaw is failing to account for natural fluctuations.
  a. Depth
  b. Differential
  c. Degrees of freedom
  d. Regression

43. _____ is the likelihood or chance that something is the case or will happen. Theoretical _____ is used extensively in areas such as statistics, mathematics, science and philosophy to draw conclusions about the likelihood of potential events and the underlying mechanics of complex systems.

The word _____ does not have a consistent direct definition.

  a. Standardized moment
  b. Discrete random variable
  c. Statistical significance
  d. Probability

44. The word _____ has many distinct meanings in different fields of knowledge, depending on their methodologies and the context of discussion. Broadly speaking we can say that a _____ is some kind of belief or claim that (supposedly) explains, asserts, or consolidates some class of claims. Additionally, in contrast with a theorem the statement of the _____ is generally accepted only in some tentative fashion as opposed to regarding it as having been conclusively established.
   a. Per mil
   b. Defined
   c. Transport of structure
   d. Theory

45. The method of _____ or ordinary _____ is used to solve overdetermined systems. _____ is often applied in statistical contexts, particularly regression analysis.

   _____ can be interpreted as a method of fitting data.

   a. System equivalence
   b. Rata Die
   c. Non-linear least squares
   d. Least squares

46. In signal processing, _____ is the reduction of a continuous signal to a discrete signal. A common example is the conversion of a sound wave to a sequence of samples.

   A sample refers to a value or set of values at a point in time and/or space.

   a. Disk
   b. Decidable
   c. Converse logic
   d. Sampling

47. The _____ is a statistic expressing the amount of random sampling error in a survey's results. The larger the _____, the less faith one should have that the poll's reported results are close to the 'true' figures; that is, the figures for the whole population.

   The _____ is usually defined as the 'radius' of a confidence interval for a particular statistic from a survey.

   a. Margin of error
   b. Conditional variance
   c. Squared deviations
   d. Moment about the mean

48. _____ is a special mathematical relationship between two quantities. Two quantities are called proportional if they vary in such a way that one of the quantities is a constant multiple of the other, or equivalently if they have a constant ratio.
   a. Depth
   b. Discontinuity
   c. Compression
   d. Proportionality

49. _____ is a fee, paid on borrowed capital. Assets lent include money, shares, consumer goods through hire purchase, major assets such as aircraft, and even entire factories in finance lease arrangements. The _____ is calculated upon the value of the assets in the same manner as upon money.
   a. A Mathematical Theory of Communication
   b. Interest expense
   c. Interest sensitivity gap
   d. Interest

Chapter 4. STATISTICS

50. Following a statistical study, a layman may well ask: 'How much _____ can we have in these conclusions?'. A problem immediately arises because a statistician's technical understanding of the term '_____' can differ radically from a layperson's.

The question 'how much _____ can we have in these conclusions?' can have several ramifications, some of which are:

- how reliable are the individual items of data being analysed: do the values measure what they are supposed to measure?
- how extensive is the dataset?
- how representative of the target population is the sample selected?
- how accurately can the important quantities be estimated from the dataset?
- if testing that an intervention has an effect, what is the smallest size of effect that could reliably have been detected from such a dataset as was available.

The last two questions correspond broadly to outcomes of statistical analyses using _____ intervals and examining the statistical power of a test, but careful interpretation is needed. Other statistical approches to these questions are available.

a. 2-3 heap
b. 120-cell
c. 1-center problem
d. Confidence

51. A _____ is an abstract model that uses mathematical language to describe the behavior of a system. Eykhoff defined a _____ as 'a representation of the essential aspects of an existing system which presents knowledge of that system in usable form'.

a. Mathematical model
b. Metaheuristic
c. Total least squares
d. Rata Die

52. A quadratic equation with real solutions, called roots, which may be real or complex, is given by the _____: $x = \frac{-b \pm \sqrt{b^2 - 4ac}}{2a}$.

a. Parametric continuity
b. Differential Algebra
c. Quotient
d. Quadratic formula

53. In mathematics, a _____ is a constant multiplicative factor of a certain object. For example, in the expression $9x^2$, the _____ of x^2 is 9.

The object can be such things as a variable, a vector, a function, etc.

a. Fibonacci polynomials
b. Multivariate division algorithm
c. Stability radius
d. Coefficient

54. In probability theory and statistics, _____ indicates the strength and direction of a linear relationship between two random variables. That is in contrast with the usage of the term in colloquial speech, denoting any relationship, not necessarily linear. In general statistical usage, _____ or co-relation refers to the departure of two random variables from independence.

a. Correlation
b. Summary statistics
c. Random variables
d. Sample size

55. The term '_____' refers to the concept of collecting information and attempting to spot a pattern in the information. In some fields of study, the term '_____' has more formally-defined meanings.

Although _____ is often used to predict future events, it could be used to estimate uncertain events in the past, such as how many ancient kings probably ruled between two dates, based on data such as the average years which other known kings reigned.

a. Trend analysis
b. Probit model
c. Partial least squares
d. Partial leverage

56. In mathematics, the _____ is an approach to finding a particular solution to certain inhomogeneous ordinary differential equations and recurrence relations. It is closely related to the annihilator method, but instead of using a particular kind of differential operator in order to find the best possible form of the particular solution, a 'guess' is made as to the appropriate form, which is then tested by differentiating the resulting equation. In this sense, the _____ is less formal but more intuitive than the annihilator method.

a. Differential algebraic equations
b. Phase line
c. Linear differential equation
d. Method of undetermined coefficients

57. A _____ is a 2D geometric symbolic representation of information according to some visualization technique. Sometimes, the technique uses a 3D visualization which is then projected onto the 2D surface. The word graph is sometimes used as a synonym for _____.

a. 120-cell
b. 2-3 heap
c. Diagram
d. 1-center problem

Chapter 5. FINANCE

1. In mathematics, _____ and undefined are used to explain whether or not expressions have meaningful, sensible, and unambiguous values. Not all branches of mathematics come to the same conclusion.

The following expressions are undefined in all contexts, but remarks in the analysis section may apply.

   a. Plugging in
   b. LHS
   c. Toy model
   d. Defined

2. _____ is a fee, paid on borrowed capital. Assets lent include money, shares, consumer goods through hire purchase, major assets such as aircraft, and even entire factories in finance lease arrangements. The _____ is calculated upon the value of the assets in the same manner as upon money.
   a. Interest
   b. Interest sensitivity gap
   c. A Mathematical Theory of Communication
   d. Interest expense

3. _____ is the concept of adding accumulated interest back to the principal, so that interest is earned on interest from that moment on. The act of declaring interest to be principal is called compounding. A loan, for example, may have its interest compounded every month: in this case, a loan with $100 principal and 1% interest per month would have a balance of $101 at the end of the first month.
   a. Compound interest
   b. Retained interest
   c. Net interest margin securities
   d. Net interest margin

4. In abstract algebra, a module S over a ring R is called _____ or irreducible if it is not the zero module 0 and if its only submodules are 0 and S. Understanding the _____ modules over a ring is usually helpful because these modules form the 'building blocks' of all other modules in a certain sense.

Abelian groups are the same as Z-modules.

   a. Derivation
   b. Simple
   c. Basis
   d. Harmonic series

5. _____ is a quantity expressing the two-dimensional size of a defined part of a surface, typically a region bounded by a closed curve. The term surface _____ refers to the total _____ of the exposed surface of a 3-dimensional solid, such as the sum of the _____s of the exposed sides of a polyhedron. _____ is an important invariant in the differential geometry of surfaces.
   a. A chemical equation
   b. A posteriori
   c. A Mathematical Theory of Communication
   d. Area

6. A _____ is a device for performing mathematical calculations, distinguished from a computer by having a limited problem solving ability and an interface optimized for interactive calculation rather than programming. _____s can be hardware or software, and mechanical or electronic, and are often built into devices such as PDAs or mobile phones.

Modern electronic _____s are generally small, digital, and usually inexpensive.

   a. 120-cell
   b. 2-3 heap
   c. 1-center problem
   d. Calculator

Chapter 5. FINANCE

7. In mathematics and in the sciences, a _____ (plural: _____e, formulæ or _____s) is a concise way of expressing information symbolically (as in a mathematical or chemical _____), or a general relationship between quantities. One of many famous _____e is Albert Einstein's E = mc² (see special relativity

In mathematics, a _____ is a key to solve an equation with variables. For example, the problem of determining the volume of a sphere is one that requires a significant amount of integral calculus to solve.

- a. 1-center problem
- b. 120-cell
- c. 2-3 heap
- d. Formula

8. A _____ typically refers to a class of handheld calculators that are capable of plotting graphs, solving simultaneous equations, and performing numerous other tasks with variables. Most popular _____s are also programmable, allowing the user to create customized programs, typically for scientific/engineering and education applications. Due to their large displays intended for graphing, they can also accommodate several lines of text and calculations at a time.
- a. Graphing calculator
- b. Bump mapping
- c. Support vector machines
- d. Genus

9. In mathematics, a _____ is a way of expressing a number as a fraction of 100. It is often denoted using the percent sign, '%'. For example, 45% is equal to 45 / 100, or 0.45.
- a. Lowest common denominator
- b. Subtrahend
- c. Least common multiple
- d. Percentage

10. A _____ is one of the basic shapes of geometry: a polygon with three corners or vertices and three sides or edges which are line segments. A _____ with vertices A, B, and C is denoted ABC.

In Euclidean geometry any three non-collinear points determine a unique _____ and a unique plane.

- a. Fuhrmann circle
- b. 1-center problem
- c. Kepler triangle
- d. Triangle

11. _____ is that which is owed; usually referencing assets owed, but the term can cover other obligations. In the case of assets, _____ is a means of using future purchasing power in the present before a summation has been earned.
- a. Cobb-Douglas
- b. Debt
- c. Metaheuristic
- d. Point-slope form

12. In mathematics, an _____, or central tendency of a data set refers to a measure of the 'middle' or 'expected' value of the data set. There are many different descriptive statistics that can be chosen as a measurement of the central tendency of the data items.

An _____ is a single value that is meant to typify a list of values.

- a. A chemical equation
- b. A posteriori
- c. A Mathematical Theory of Communication
- d. Average

13. The _____ is the period of time required for a quantity to double in size or value.

Chapter 5. FINANCE

a. Zenzizenzizenzic
c. Power law
b. Stretched exponential function
d. Doubling time

14. _____ or amortisation is the process of decreasing an amount over a period of time. The word comes from Middle English amortisen to kill, alienate in mortmain, from Anglo-French amorteser, alteration of amortir, from Vulgar Latin admortire to kill, from Latin ad- + mort-, mors death. Particular instances of the term include:

- _____, the allocation of a lump sum amount to different time periods, particularly for loans and other forms of finance, including related interest or other finance charges.
    - _____ schedule, a table detailing each periodic payment on a loan, as generated by an _____ calculator.
    - Negative _____, an _____ schedule where the loan amount actually increases through not paying the full interest
- Amortized analysis, analyzing the execution cost of algorithms over a sequence of operations.
- _____ of capital expenditures of certain assets under accounting rules, particularly intangible assets, in a manner analogous to depreciation.
- _____

_____ is also used in the context of zoning regulations and describes the time in which a property owner has to relocate when the property's use constitutes a preexisting nonconforming use under zoning regulations.

- Depreciation

a. Amortization
c. Identity
b. Origin
d. ISAAC

15. An _____ is a table detailing each periodic payment on a amortizing loan, as generated by an amortization calculator.

While a portion of every payment is applied towards both the interest and the principal balance of the loan, the exact amount applied to principal each time varies. An _____ reveals the specific monetary amount put towards interest, as well as the specific put towards the Principal balance, with each payment.

a. Accounts receivable
c. Amortization schedule
b. A Mathematical Theory of Communication
d. A chemical equation

16. In computational complexity theory, an algorithm is said to take _____ if the asymptotic upper bound for the time it requires is proportional to the size of the input, which is usually denoted n.

Informally spoken, the running time increases linearly with the size of the input. For example, a procedure that adds up all elements of a list requires time proportional to the length of the list.

a. Truth table reduction
c. Time-constructible function
b. Linear time
d. Constructible function

Chapter 5. FINANCE

17. In mathematics, a _____ is a number that can be expressed as an integral of an algebraic function over an algebraic domain. Kontsevich and Zagier define a _____ as a complex number whose real and imaginary parts are values of absolutely convergent integrals of rational functions with rational coefficients, over domains in given by polynomial inequalities with rational coefficients.
    a. Boussinesq approximation
    b. Period
    c. Closeness
    d. Disk

18. An angle smaller than a right angle is called an _____ (less than 90 degrees).
    a. Euclidean geometry
    b. Ultraparallel theorem
    c. Integral geometry
    d. Acute angle

19. In geometry and trigonometry, an _____ is the figure formed by two rays sharing a common endpoint, called the vertex of the _____. The magnitude of the _____ is the 'amount of rotation' that separates the two rays, and can be measured by considering the length of circular arc swept out when one ray is rotated about the vertex to coincide with the other. Where there is no possibility of confusion, the term '_____' is used interchangeably for both the geometric configuration itself and for its angular magnitude.
    a. Angle
    b. A Mathematical Theory of Communication
    c. A chemical equation
    d. A posteriori

20. A _____ is the transfer of an interest in property (or in law the equivalent - a charge) to a lender as a security for a debt - usually a loan of money. While a _____ in itself is not a debt, it is lender's security for a debt. It is a transfer of an interest in land (or the equivalent), from the owner to the _____ lender, on the condition that this interest will be returned to the owner of the real estate when the terms of the _____ have been satisfied or performed.
    a. 2-3 heap
    b. 120-cell
    c. 1-center problem
    d. Mortgage

21. The terms _____, nominal APR, and effective APR describe the interest rate for a whole year, rather than just a monthly fee/rate, as applied on a loan, mortgage, credit card, etc. Those terms have formal, legal definitions in some countries or legal jurisdictions, but in general:

    - The nominal APR is the simple-interest rate.
    - The effective APR is the fee+compound interest rate.

The nominal APR is calculated as: the rate, for a payment period, multiplied by the number of payment periods in a year. However, the exact legal definition of 'effective APR' can vary greatly in each jurisdiction, depending on the type of fees included, such as participation fees, loan origination fees, monthly service charges, or late fees. The effective APR has been called the 'mathematically-true' interest rate for each year. The computation for the effective APR, as the fee+compound interest rate, can also vary depending on whether the up-front fees, such as origination or participation fees, are added to the entire amount, or treated as a short-term loan due in the first payment.

   a. A posteriori
   b. A chemical equation
   c. A Mathematical Theory of Communication
   d. Annual percentage rate

22. _____ is the calculated approximation of a result which is usable even if input data may be incomplete or uncertain.

In statistics, see _____ theory, estimator.

In mathematics, approximation or _____ typically means finding upper or lower bounds of a quantity that cannot readily be computed precisely and is also an educated guess.

a. Estimator
c. Estimation theory

b. Estimation
d. U-statistic

Chapter 6. VOTING AND APPORTIONMENT

1. The _____ is a single-winner election method in which voters rank candidates in order of preference. The _____ determines the winner of an election by giving each candidate a certain number of points corresponding to the position in which he or she is ranked by each voter. Once all votes have been counted the candidate with the most points is the winner.

   a. 2-3 heap
   b. 1-center problem
   c. 120-cell
   d. Borda count

2. In mathematics, a _____ is a statement that can be proved on the basis of explicitly stated or previously agreed assumptions.

   a. Disjunction introduction
   b. Theorem
   c. Boolean function
   d. Logical value

3. In mathematics, _____ and undefined are used to explain whether or not expressions have meaningful, sensible, and unambiguous values. Not all branches of mathematics come to the same conclusion.

   The following expressions are undefined in all contexts, but remarks in the analysis section may apply.

   a. Toy model
   b. LHS
   c. Plugging in
   d. Defined

4. In mathematics, a _____ of an integer n is an integer which evenly divides n without leaving a remainder.

   For example, 7 is a _____ of 42 because 42/7 = 6. We also say 42 is divisible by 7 or 42 is a multiple of 7 or 7 divides 42 or 7 is a factor of 42 and we usually write 7 | 42.

   a. 2-3 heap
   b. 1-center problem
   c. 120-cell
   d. Divisor

5. _____ is the study of terms and their use. Terms are words and compound words that are used in specific contexts. Not to be confused with 'terms' in colloquial usages, the shortened form of technical terms which are defined within a discipline or specialty field.

   a. Terminology
   b. 1-center problem
   c. 120-cell
   d. 2-3 heap

6. In statistics, _____ has two related meanings:

   - the arithmetic _____.
   - the expected value of a random variable, which is also called the population _____.

   It is sometimes stated that the '_____' _____s average. This is incorrect if '_____' is taken in the specific sense of 'arithmetic _____' as there are different types of averages: the _____, median, and mode. For instance, average house prices almost always use the median value for the average.

   For a real-valued random variable X, the _____ is the expectation of X.

Chapter 6. VOTING AND APPORTIONMENT

a. Proportional hazards model
b. Statistical population
c. Probability
d. Mean

7. In mathematics and statistics, the _____ of a list of numbers is the sum of all of the list divided by the number of items in the list. If the list is a statistical population, then the mean of that population is called a population mean. If the list is a statistical sample, we call the resulting statistic a sample mean.

a. Unsolved problems in statistics
b. Interval estimation
c. Arithmetic mean
d. Analysis of variance

8. The _____, in mathematics, is a type of mean or average, which indicates the central tendency or typical value of a set of numbers. It is similar to the arithmetic mean, which is what most people think of with the word 'average,' except that instead of adding the set of numbers and then dividing the sum by the count of numbers in the set, n, the numbers are multiplied and then the nth root of the resulting product is taken.

For instance, the _____ of two numbers, say 2 and 8, is just the square root (i.e., the second root) of their product, 16, which is 4.

a. Skewness
b. Correlation
c. Stratified sampling
d. Geometric mean

9. The _____ was the first of the apportionment paradoxes to be discovered. The US House of Representatives is Constitutionally required to allocate seats based on population counts, which are required every 10 years. The size of the House is set by statute.

a. Infinity
b. Alabama paradox
c. A Mathematical Theory of Communication
d. Implicit differentiation

Chapter 7. NUMBER SYSTEMS AND NUMBER THEORY

1. In mathematics, a _____ is a set of numbers,, together with one or more operations, such as addition or multiplication.

Examples of _____s include: natural numbers, integers, rational numbers, algebraic numbers, real numbers, complex numbers, p-adic numbers, surreal numbers, and hyperreal numbers.

   a. Slope
   b. Number System
   c. Tally marks
   d. Number line

2. _____ is the branch of pure mathematics concerned with the properties of numbers in general, and integers in particular, as well as the wider classes of problems that arise from their study.

_____ may be subdivided into several fields, according to the methods used and the type of questions investigated.

The term 'arithmetic' is also used to refer to _____.

   a. Goormaghtigh conjecture
   b. Coin problem
   c. Sociable number
   d. Number Theory

3. The word _____ has many distinct meanings in different fields of knowledge, depending on their methodologies and the context of discussion. Broadly speaking we can say that a _____ is some kind of belief or claim that (supposedly) explains, asserts, or consolidates some class of claims. Additionally, in contrast with a theorem the statement of the _____ is generally accepted only in some tentative fashion as opposed to regarding it as having been conclusively established.
   a. Per mil
   b. Defined
   c. Theory
   d. Transport of structure

4. In mathematics, _____ and undefined are used to explain whether or not expressions have meaningful, sensible, and unambiguous values. Not all branches of mathematics come to the same conclusion.

The following expressions are undefined in all contexts, but remarks in the analysis section may apply.

   a. LHS
   b. Plugging in
   c. Toy model
   d. Defined

5. In mathematics and computer science, _____ (also base-16, hexa or base, of 16. It uses sixteen distinct symbols, most often the symbols 0-9 to represent values zero to nine, and A, B, C, D, E, F (or a through f) to represent values ten to fifteen.

Its primary use is as a human friendly representation of binary coded values, so it is often used in digital electronics and computer engineering.

   a. Radix
   b. Tetradecimal
   c. Factoradic
   d. Hexadecimal

Chapter 7. NUMBER SYSTEMS AND NUMBER THEORY

6. The _____ is precursor of the abacus, and the earliest known form of a counting device (excluding fingers and other very simple methods.) _____s were made of stone or wood, and the counting was done on the board with beads, or pebbles etc. Not many boards survive because of the perishable materials used in their construction.
   a. Gibbs lemma
   b. Warsaw School of Mathematics
   c. Counting board
   d. Product order

7. The _____ is a positional numeral system; it has positions for units, tens, hundreds, etc. The position of each digit conveys the multiplier (a power of ten) to be used with that digit—each position has a value ten times that of the position to its right.
   a. Cleaver
   b. Composite
   c. Free
   d. Decimal system

8. In mathematics, computing, linguistics and related subjects, an _____ is a sequence of finite instructions, often used for calculation and data processing. It is formally a type of effective method in which a list of well-defined instructions for completing a task will, when given an initial state, proceed through a well-defined series of successive states, eventually terminating in an end-state. The transition from one state to the next is not necessarily deterministic; some _____s, known as probabilistic _____s, incorporate randomness.
   a. Approximate counting algorithm
   b. In-place algorithm
   c. Out-of-core
   d. Algorithm

9. _____ is simply the manner of writing out an expression in full. When a quantity is written as a sum of terms, or as a continued product, _____ notation is used to illustrate the expression in its entirety.
   a. Algebraic element
   b. Algebra
   c. Expanded form
   d. Algebraic function

10. _____ is a numeral system in which each position is related to the next by a constant multiplier, a common ratio, called the base or radix of that numeral system.
    a. Place value
    b. Cyrillic numerals
    c. Negative base
    d. NegaFibonacci coding

11. The _____ numeral system is the base-8 number system, and uses the digits 0 to 7. Numerals can be made from binary numerals by grouping consecutive digits into groups of three (starting from the right.) For example, the binary representation for decimal 74 is 1001010, which groups into 001 001 010 -- so the _____ representation is 112.
    a. A posteriori
    b. A chemical equation
    c. A Mathematical Theory of Communication
    d. Octal

12. The _____ is the apparent path that the Sun traces out in the sky during the year. As it appears to move in the sky in relation to the stars, the apparent path aligns with the planets throughout the course of the year. More accurately, it is the intersection of a spherical surface, the celestial sphere, with the _____ plane, which is the geometric plane containing the mean orbit of the Earth around the Sun.
    a. A chemical equation
    b. Ecliptic
    c. Escape velocity
    d. A Mathematical Theory of Communication

Chapter 7. NUMBER SYSTEMS AND NUMBER THEORY

13. In commutative and homological algebra, _____ is an important invariant of rings and modules. Although _____ can be defined more generally, the most common case considered is the case of modules over a commutative Noetherian local ring. In this case, the _____ of a module is related with its projective dimension by the Auslander-Buchsbaum formula.
    a. Closed form
    b. Basis
    c. Closeness
    d. Depth

14. An _____ is an artifact, usually two-dimensional (a picture), that has a similar appearance to some subject--usually a physical object or a person.

    _____s may be two-dimensional, such as a photograph, screen display, and as well as a three-dimensional, such as a statue. They may be captured by optical devices--such as cameras, mirrors, lenses, telescopes, microscopes, etc.

    a. A Mathematical Theory of Communication
    b. A chemical equation
    c. A posteriori
    d. Image

15. _____ is the mathematical operation of scaling one number by another. It is one of the four basic operations in elementary arithmetic.

    _____ is defined for whole numbers in terms of repeated addition; for example, 4 multiplied by 3 can be calculated by adding 3 copies of 4 together:

    $$4 + 4 + 4 = 12.$$

    _____ of rational numbers and real numbers is defined by systematic generalization of this basic idea.

    a. Multiplication
    b. Highest common factor
    c. Least common multiple
    d. The number 0 is even.

16. A _____ number is a positive integer which has a positive divisor other than one or itself. By definition, every integer greater than one is either a prime number or a _____ number. zero and one are considered to be neither prime nor _____. For example, the integer 14 is a _____ number because it can be factored as 2 × 7.
    a. Basis
    b. Key server
    c. Discontinuity
    d. Composite

17. A _____ is a positive integer which has a positive divisor other than one or itself. In other words, if 0 < n is an integer and there are integers 1 < a, b < n such that n = a × b then n is composite. By definition, every integer greater than one is either a prime number or a _____.
    a. Ruth-Aaron pair
    b. Megaprime
    c. Composite number
    d. Prime Pages

18. In mathematics, a _____ can mean either an element of the set {1, 2, 3, ...} or an element of the set {0, 1, 2, 3, ...}. The latter is especially preferred in mathematical logic, set theory, and computer science.

    _____s have two main purposes: they can be used for counting, and they can be used for ordering.

Chapter 7. NUMBER SYSTEMS AND NUMBER THEORY

a. Cardinal numbers
c. Natural number
b. Strong partition cardinal
d. Suslin cardinal

19. In mathematics, a _____ is a natural number which has exactly two distinct natural number divisors: 1 and itself. An infinitude of _____s exists, as demonstrated by Euclid around 300 BC. The first twenty-five _____s are:

2, 3, 5, 7, 11, 13, 17, 19, 23, 29, 31, 37, 41, 43, 47, 53, 59, 61, 67, 71, 73, 79, 83, 89, 97.

a. Perrin number
c. Highly composite number
b. Prime number
d. Pronic number

20. In mathematics, in the realm of group theory, a group is said to be _____ if it equals its own commutator subgroup if the group has no nontrivial abelian quotients.

The smallest _____ group is the alternating group A_5. More generally, any non-abelian simple group is _____ since the commutator subgroup is a normal subgroup with abelian quotient.

a. Group of Lie type
c. Perfect
b. Quaternion group
d. Free product

21. In mathematics, a _____ is defined as a positive integer which is the sum of its proper positive divisors, that is, the sum of the positive divisors excluding the number itself. Equivalently, a _____ is a number that is half the sum of all of its positive divisors, or = 2n.

The first _____ is 6, because 1, 2, and 3 are its proper positive divisors, and 1 + 2 + 3 = 6.

a. Blum integer
c. Nonhypotenuse number
b. Perfect number
d. Leonardo numbers

22. In mathematics, the _____ is a simple, ancient algorithm for finding all prime numbers up to a specified integer. It works efficiently for the smaller primes . It was created by Eratosthenes, an ancient Greek mathematician.
a. 120-cell
c. 1-center problem
b. 2-3 heap
d. Sieve of Eratosthenes

23. _____ IPA: [pjÉ›Ë Ê dÉ™fÉ›Ê 'ma] (17 August 1601 or 1607/8 - 12 January 1665) was a French lawyer at the Parlement of Toulouse, France, and a mathematician who is given credit for early developments that led to modern calculus. In particular, he is recognized for his discovery of an original method of finding the greatest and the smallest ordinates of curved lines, which is analogous to that of the then unknown differential calculus, as well as his research into the theory of numbers. He also made notable contributions to analytic geometry, probability, and optics.
a. Philip J. Davis
c. Felix Hausdorff
b. Nikita Borisov
d. Pierre de Fermat

24. In cryptography, _____ is the process of transforming information using an algorithm to make it unreadable to anyone except those possessing special knowledge, usually referred to as a key. The result of the process is encrypted information. In many contexts, the word _____ also implicitly refers to the reverse process, decryption, to make the encrypted information readable again.

a. One-time pad
b. End-to-end encryption
c. Authenticated encryption
d. Encryption

25. In mathematics, a Mersenne number is a positive integer that is one less than a power of two:

$$M_n = 2^n - 1.$$

Some definitions of Mersenne numbers require that the exponent n be prime.

A _____ is a Mersenne number that is prime. As of October 2008, only 46 _____s are known; the largest known prime number ($2^{43,112,609} - 1$) is a _____, and in modern times, the largest known prime has almost always been a _____.

a. Mersenne number
b. 1-center problem
c. Mersenne prime
d. Red-black tree

26. In mathematics, an _____ or excessive number is a number n for which σσ− 2n is called the abundance of n.
a. Idoneal number
b. Integer sequence
c. Unitary perfect number
d. Abundant number

27. In mathematics, a _____ or defective number is a number n for which σσ
a. Highly totient number
b. Woodall number
c. Kynea number
d. Deficient number

28. A _____ is a simple shape of Euclidean geometry consisting of those points in a plane which are at a constant distance, called the radius, from a fixed point, called the center. A _____ with center A is sometimes denoted by the symbol A.

A chord of a _____ is a line segment whose two endpoints lie on the _____.

a. Circular segment
b. Circle
c. Circumcircle
d. Malfatti circles

29. Leonardo of Pisa (c. 1170 - c. 1250), also known as Leonardo Pisano, Leonardo Bonacci, Leonardo _____, or, most commonly, simply _____, was an Italian mathematician, considered by some 'the most talented mathematician of the Middle Ages'.
a. Fibonacci
b. Guido Castelnuovo
c. Harry Hinsley
d. Ralph C. Merkle

30. In mathematics, the _____ are a sequence of numbers named after Leonardo of Pisa, known as Fibonacci. Fibonacci's 1202 book Liber Abaci introduced the sequence to Western European mathematics, although the sequence had been previously described in Indian mathematics.

Chapter 7. NUMBER SYSTEMS AND NUMBER THEORY 61

The first number of the sequence is 0, the second number is 1, and each subsequent number is equal to the sum of the previous two numbers of the sequence itself, yielding the sequence 0, 1, 1, 2, 3, 5, 8, etc.

- a. Fibonacci numbers
- b. Lucas pseudoprime
- c. 1-center problem
- d. Pisano period

31. In mathematics and the arts, two quantities are in the _____ if the ratio between the sum of those quantities and the larger one is the same as the ratio between the larger one and the smaller. The _____ is an irrational mathematical constant, approximately 1.6180339887.

At least since the Renaissance, many artists and architects have proportioned their works to approximate the _____ -- especially in the form of the golden rectangle, in which the ratio of the longer side to the shorter is the _____ --believing this proportion to be aesthetically pleasing.

- a. Golden ratio
- b. 2-3 heap
- c. 1-center problem
- d. 120-cell

32. In mathematics, a _____ is a curve which emanates from a central point, getting progressively farther away as it revolves around the point. An Archimedean _____, a helix, and a conic _____.

A '_____' and a 'helix' are two terms that are easily confused, but represent different objects.

A _____ is typically a planar curve, like the groove on a record or the arms of a _____ galaxy.

- a. Logarithmic spiral
- b. Spiral
- c. Fresnel integrals
- d. Cornu spiral

33. In geometry, a _____ is defined as a quadrilateral where all four of its angles are right angles.
- a. Point group in two dimensions
- b. Cantor-Dedekind axiom
- c. Polytope
- d. Rectangle

34. _____ is a special mathematical relationship between two quantities. Two quantities are called proportional if they vary in such a way that one of the quantities is a constant multiple of the other, or equivalently if they have a constant ratio.
- a. Discontinuity
- b. Compression
- c. Depth
- d. Proportionality

35. In mathematics and in the sciences, a _____ (plural: _____e, formulæ or _____s) is a concise way of expressing information symbolically (as in a mathematical or chemical _____), or a general relationship between quantities. One of many famous _____e is Albert Einstein's $E = mc^2$ (see special relativity

In mathematics, a _____ is a key to solve an equation with variables. For example, the problem of determining the volume of a sphere is one that requires a significant amount of integral calculus to solve.

a. 120-cell
b. 2-3 heap
c. 1-center problem
d. Formula

Chapter 8. GEOMETRY

1. In mathematics, an _____ or member of a set is any one of the distinct objects that make up that set.

Writing A = {1,2,3,4}, means that the _____s of the set A are the numbers 1, 2, 3 and 4. Groups of _____s of A, for example {1,2}, are subsets of A.

a. Order
c. Universal code

b. Element
d. Ideal

2. _____ IPA: [pjɛːʁ dɛˑfɛːʁ 'ma] (17 August 1601 or 1607/8 - 12 January 1665) was a French lawyer at the Parlement of Toulouse, France, and a mathematician who is given credit for early developments that led to modern calculus. In particular, he is recognized for his discovery of an original method of finding the greatest and the smallest ordinates of curved lines, which is analogous to that of the then unknown differential calculus, as well as his research into the theory of numbers. He also made notable contributions to analytic geometry, probability, and optics.

a. Pierre de Fermat
c. Philip J. Davis

b. Nikita Borisov
d. Felix Hausdorff

3. A _____ is generally 'a rough or fragmented geometric shape that can be split into parts, each of which is a reduced-size copy of the whole,' a property called self-similarity. The term was coined by Benoît Mandelbrot in 1975 and was derived from the Latin fractus meaning 'broken' or 'fractured.' A mathematical _____ is based on an equation that undergoes iteration, a form of feedback based on recursion.

A _____ often has the following features:

- It has a fine structure at arbitrarily small scales.
- It is too irregular to be easily described in traditional Euclidean geometric language.
- It is self-similar.
- It has a Hausdorff dimension which is greater than its topological dimension.
- It has a simple and recursive definition.

Because they appear similar at all levels of magnification, _____s are often considered to be infinitely complex. Natural objects that approximate _____s to a degree include clouds, mountain ranges, lightning bolts, coastlines, and snow flakes.

a. Zero-point energy
c. Cube

b. Logical disjunction
d. Fractal

4. _____ is a part of mathematics concerned with questions of size, shape, and relative position of figures and with properties of space. _____ is one of the oldest sciences. Initially a body of practical knowledge concerning lengths, areas, and volumes, in the third century BC _____ was put into an axiomatic form by Euclid, whose treatment--Euclidean _____--set a standard for many centuries to follow.

a. 120-cell
c. 1-center problem

b. 2-3 heap
d. Geometry

5. In mathematics, a _____ is a convincing demonstration that some mathematical statement is necessarily true. _____s are obtained from deductive reasoning, rather than from inductive or empirical arguments. That is, a _____ must demonstrate that a statement is true in all cases, without a single exception.

a. Conchoid
b. Congruent
c. Proof
d. Germ

6. _____ is a quantity expressing the two-dimensional size of a defined part of a surface, typically a region bounded by a closed curve. The term surface _____ refers to the total _____ of the exposed surface of a 3-dimensional solid, such as the sum of the _____ s of the exposed sides of a polyhedron. _____ is an important invariant in the differential geometry of surfaces.
   a. Area
   b. A posteriori
   c. A chemical equation
   d. A Mathematical Theory of Communication

7. In geometry, a _____ is a polygon with six edges and six vertices. A regular _____ has Schläfli symbol {6}. The internal angles of a regular _____ are all 120° and the _____ has 720 degrees.
   a. Polygonal curve
   b. Decagon
   c. Polygonal chain
   d. Hexagon

8. The _____ is a mathematical curve and one of the earliest fractal curves to have been described. It appeared in a 1904 paper entitled "On a continuous curve without tangents constructible from elementary geometry" by the Swedish mathematician Helge von Koch.
   a. 120-cell
   b. 1-center problem
   c. 2-3 heap
   d. Koch snowflake

9. In geometry, an _____ is a polygon that has eight sides. A regular _____ is represented by the Schläfli symbol {8}. A regular _____ is constructible with compass and straightedge.
   a. Enneagon
   b. Octagon
   c. A Mathematical Theory of Communication
   d. Equilateral polygon

10. In geometry, a _____ is any five-sided polygon. A _____ may be simple or self-intersecting. The internal angles in a simple _____ total 540°.
    a. Star polygon
    b. Regular octagon
    c. Triskaidecagon
    d. Pentagon

11. The _____ is the length of the line that bounds an area In the special case where the area is circular, the _____ is known as the circumference.
    a. Concyclic
    b. Perimeter
    c. Multilateration
    d. Reflection symmetry

12. In geometry a _____ is traditionally a plane figure that is bounded by a closed path or circuit, composed of a finite sequence of straight line segments. These segments are called its edges or sides, and the points where two edges meet are the _____'s vertices or corners. The interior of the _____ is sometimes called its body.
    a. Polygonal curve
    b. Regular polygon
    c. Parallelogon
    d. Polygon

Chapter 8. GEOMETRY

13. _____ are used in computer graphics to compose images that are three-dimensional in appearance. Usually triangular, _____ arise when an object's surface is modeled, vertices are selected, and the object is rendered in a wire frame model. This is quicker to display than a shaded model; thus the _____ are a stage in computer animation.
    a. Triskaidecagon
    b. Visibility polygon
    c. Heptadecagon
    d. Polygons

14. In geometry, a _____ is a polygon with four sides or edges and four vertices or corners. Sometimes, the term quadrangle is used, for etymological symmetry with triangle, and sometimes tetragon for consistency with pentagon, hexagon and so on. The interior angles of a _____ add up to 360 degrees of arc.
    a. 1-center problem
    b. 120-cell
    c. Quadrilateral
    d. 2-3 heap

15. In mathematics, _____ and undefined are used to explain whether or not expressions have meaningful, sensible, and unambiguous values. Not all branches of mathematics come to the same conclusion.

The following expressions are undefined in all contexts, but remarks in the analysis section may apply.

    a. Toy model
    b. Plugging in
    c. LHS
    d. Defined

16. In geometry, a _____ is a quadrilateral with two sets of parallel sides. The opposite sides of a _____ are of equal length, and the opposite angles of a _____ are congruent. The three-dimensional counterpart of a _____ is a parallelepiped.
    a. 1-center problem
    b. 120-cell
    c. 2-3 heap
    d. Parallelogram

17. In geometry, a _____ is defined as a quadrilateral where all four of its angles are right angles.
    a. Cantor-Dedekind axiom
    b. Rectangle
    c. Polytope
    d. Point group in two dimensions

18. A _____ or a trapezium is a quadrilateral that has at least one pair of parallel lines for sides.

Some authors define it as a quadrilateral having exactly one pair of parallel sides, so as to exclude parallelograms, which otherwise would be regarded as a special type of _____, but most mathematicians use the inclusive definition.

In North America, the term trapezium is used to refer to a quadrilateral with no parallel sides.

    a. Lozenge
    b. Trapezoid
    c. Trapezium
    d. Rhomboid

19. In mathematics and in the sciences, a _____ (plural: _____e, formulæ or _____s) is a concise way of expressing information symbolically (as in a mathematical or chemical _____), or a general relationship between quantities. One of many famous _____e is Albert Einstein's $E = mc^2$ (see special relativity

In mathematics, a _____ is a key to solve an equation with variables. For example, the problem of determining the volume of a sphere is one that requires a significant amount of integral calculus to solve.

   a. 1-center problem
   c. 2-3 heap
   b. Formula
   d. 120-cell

20. A _____ is one of the basic shapes of geometry: a polygon with three corners or vertices and three sides or edges which are line segments. A _____ with vertices A, B, and C is denoted ABC.

In Euclidean geometry any three non-collinear points determine a unique _____ and a unique plane.

   a. Fuhrmann circle
   c. Kepler triangle
   b. 1-center problem
   d. Triangle

21. A _____ is the longest side of a right triangle, the side opposite of the right angle. The length of the _____ of a right triangle can be found using the Pythagorean theorem, which states that the square of the length of the _____ equals the sum of the squares of the lengths of the two other sides.

For example, if one of the other sides has a length of 3 meters and the other has a length of 4 m.

   a. Concyclic points
   c. Hypotenuse
   b. Golden angle
   d. Reflection symmetry

22. In a right triangle, the cathetusoriginally from the Greek word Κῆθετος, plural catheti

   - 1 Generally
   - 2 References
   - 3 See also
   - 4 External links

In a wider sense, a _____ is any line falling perpendicularly on another line or a surface. Such a line is more commonly known as a surface normal.

   a. Face diagonal
   c. Line segment
   b. Central angle
   d. Cathetus

23. In mathematics, the _____ or Pythagoras' theorem is a relation in Euclidean geometry among the three sides of a right triangle. The theorem is named after the Greek mathematician Pythagoras, who by tradition is credited with its discovery and proof, although it is often argued that knowledge of the theory predates him.. The theorem is as follows:

In any right triangle, the area of the square whose side is the hypotenuse is equal to the sum of the areas of the squares whose sides are the two legs.

a. 2-3 heap
b. 120-cell
c. 1-center problem
d. Pythagorean Theorem

24. In mathematics, a _____ is a statement that can be proved on the basis of explicitly stated or previously agreed assumptions.
a. Logical value
b. Boolean function
c. Disjunction introduction
d. Theorem

25. The term _____ or centre is used in various contexts in abstract algebra to denote the set of all those elements that commute with all other elements. More specifically:

- The _____ of a group G consists of all those elements x in G such that xg = gx for all g in G. This is a normal subgroup of G.
- The _____ of a ring R is the subset of R consisting of all those elements x of R such that xr = rx for all r in R. The _____ is a commutative subring of R, so R is an algebra over its _____.
- The _____ of an algebra A consists of all those elements x of A such that xa = ax for all a in A. See also: central simple algebra.
- The _____ of a Lie algebra L consists of all those elements x in L such that [x,a] = 0 for all a in L. This is an ideal of the Lie algebra L.
- The _____ of a monoidal category C consists of pairs *a natural isomorphism satisfying certain axioms*.

a. Brute Force
b. Center
c. Block size
d. Disk

26. A _____ is a simple shape of Euclidean geometry consisting of those points in a plane which are at a constant distance, called the radius, from a fixed point, called the center. A _____ with center A is sometimes denoted by the symbol A.

A chord of a _____ is a line segment whose two endpoints lie on the _____.

a. Circular segment
b. Circumcircle
c. Malfatti circles
d. Circle

27. In classical geometry, a _____ of a circle or sphere is any line segment from its center to its boundary. By extension, the _____ of a circle or sphere is the length of any such segment. The _____ is half the diameter. In science and engineering the term _____ of curvature is commonly used as a synonym for _____.
a. Birational geometry
b. Non-Euclidean geometry
c. Duoprism
d. Radius

28. _____ is the study of geometry using the principles of algebra. That the algebra of the real numbers can be employed to yield results about the linear continuum of geometry relies on the Cantor-Dedekind axiom. Usually the Cartesian coordinate system is applied to manipulate equations for planes, straight lines, and squares, often in two and sometimes in three dimensions of measurement.

Chapter 8. GEOMETRY

a. Angular eccentricity
c. Axis-aligned object
b. Ambient space
d. Analytic geometry

29. The _____ is the distance around a closed curve. _____ is a kind of perimeter.

The _____ of a circle is the length around it.

a. Compactness measure of a shape
c. Brascamp-Lieb inequality
b. Flatness
d. Circumference

30. The framework of quantum mechanics requires a careful definition of _____, and a thorough discussion of its practical and philosophical implications.

_____ is viewed in different ways in the many interpretations of quantum mechanics; however, despite the considerable philosophical differences, they almost universally agree on the practical question of what results from a routine quantum-physics laboratory _____. To describe this, a simple framework to use is the Copenhagen interpretation, and it will be implicitly used in this section; the utility of this approach has been verified countless times, and all other interpretations are necessarily constructed so as to give the same quantitative predictions as this in almost every case.

a. Dynamic range
c. Measurement
b. Fundamental units
d. 1-center problem

31. The _____ of any solid, plasma, vacuum or theoretical object is how much three-dimensional space it occupies, often quantified numerically. One-dimensional figures and two-dimensional shapes are assigned zero _____ in the three-dimensional space. _____ is presented as ml or cm^3.

_____s of straight-edged and circular shapes are calculated using arithmetic formulae.

a. Cauchy momentum equation
c. Thermodynamic limit
b. Stress-energy tensor
d. Volume

32. In mathematics, specifically in topology, a _____ is a two-dimensional manifold. The most familiar examples are those that arise as the boundaries of solid objects in ordinary three-dimensional Euclidean space, $E³$. On the other hand, there are also more exotic _____s, that are so 'contorted' that they cannot be embedded in three-dimensional space at all.

a. Standard torus
c. Homoeoid
b. Surface
d. Cross-cap

33. _____ is how much exposed area an object has. It is expressed in square units. If an object has flat faces, its _____ can be calculated by adding together the areas of its faces.

a. Reflection group
c. Compactness measure of a shape
b. Relative dimension
d. Surface area

34. In mathematics, a _____ is a quadric surface, with the following equation in Cartesian coordinates: $(x/a)^2 + (y/b)^2 = 1$.

Chapter 8. GEOMETRY

a. Free
b. Discontinuity
c. Derivative algebra
d. Cylinder

35. A _____ is a symmetrical geometrical object. In non-mathematical usage, the term is used to refer either to a round ball or to its two-dimensional surface. In mathematics, a _____ is the set of all points in three-dimensional space which are at distance r from a fixed point of that space, where r is a positive real number called the radius of the _____.
   a. Differential geometry of curves
   b. Lie derivative
   c. Differentiable manifold
   d. Sphere

36. A _____ is a building where the upper surfaces are triangular and converge on one point. The base of _____s are usually quadrilateral or trilateral, meaning that a _____ usually has four or five faces. A _____'s design, with the majority of the weight closer to the ground, means that less material higher up on the _____ will be pushing down from above.
   a. 120-cell
   b. 1-center problem
   c. 2-3 heap
   d. Pyramid

37. A _____ is a three-dimensional geometric shape that tapers smoothly from a flat, round base to a point called the apex or vertex. More precisely, it is the solid figure bounded by a plane base and the surface formed by the locus of all straight line segments joining the apex to the perimeter of the base. The term '_____' sometimes refers just to the surface of this solid figure, or just to the lateral surface.
   a. Gravity waves
   b. Blocking
   c. Cone
   d. Characteristic

38. The _____ is πr^2 when the circle has radius r. Here the symbol π denotes, as usual, the constant ratio of the circumference of a circle to its diameter.

Modern mathematics can obtain the area using the methods of integral calculus or its more sophisticated offspring, real analysis.

   a. Ultraparallel theorem
   b. Area of a circle
   c. A chemical equation
   d. A Mathematical Theory of Communication

39. A _____ is any one of many units of measure used by various ancient peoples and is among the first recorded units of length.

The _____ is based on measuring by comparing - especially cords and textiles, but also for timbers and stones - to one's forearm length. The Egyptian hieroglyph for the unit shows this symbol.

   a. 120-cell
   b. 2-3 heap
   c. 1-center problem
   d. Cubit

Chapter 8. GEOMETRY

40. The word _____ denotes information gained by means of observation, experience as opposed to theoretical. A central concept in science and the scientific method is that all evidence must be _____ that is, dependent on evidence or consequences that are observable by the senses. It is usually differentiated from the philosophic usage of empiricism by the use of the adjective '_____' or the adverb 'empirically.' '_____' as an adjective or adverb is used in conjunction with both the natural and social sciences, and refers to the use of working hypotheses that are testable using observation or experiment.

   a. A Mathematical Theory of Communication   b. A chemical equation
   c. Empirical   d. A posteriori

41. In traditional logic, an _____ or postulate is a proposition that is not proved or demonstrated but considered to be either self-evident, or subject to necessary decision. Therefore, its truth is taken for granted, and serves as a starting point for deducing and inferring other truths.

In mathematics, the term _____ is used in two related but distinguishable senses: 'logical _____s' and 'non-logical _____s'.

   a. AND-OR-Invert   b. Algebraic logic
   c. Enumerative definition   d. Axiom

42. In mathematics, two quantities are called _____ if they vary in such a way that one of the quantities is a constant multiple of the other, or equivalently if they have a constant ratio.

   a. 2-3 heap   b. 1-center problem
   c. 120-cell   d. Proportional

43. In geometry, two sets of points are called _____ if one can be transformed into the other by an isometry. Less formally, two figures are _____ if they have the same shape and size, but are in different positions.

In a Euclidean system, congruence is fundamental; it is the counterpart of equality for numbers.

   a. Germ   b. Gamma test
   c. Function   d. Congruent

44. In geometry, an _____ planar shape or solid is one that is enclosed by and 'fits snugly' inside another geometric shape or solid. Specifically, there must be no object similar to the _____ object but larger and also enclosed by the outer figure.

Familiar examples include circles _____ in polygons, and triangles or regular polygons _____ in circles.

   a. Inscribed   b. Equiangular polygon
   c. Omnitruncated 5-cell   d. Isometry group

45. In cryptography, _____ is a pseudorandom number generator and a stream cipher designed by Robert Jenkins to be cryptographically secure. The name is an acronym for Indirection, Shift, Accumulate, Add, and Count.

The _____ algorithm has similarities with RC4.

Chapter 8. GEOMETRY

a. Imputation
c. Order

b. Isaac
d. Introduction

46. The _____ (symbol: N) is the SI derived unit of force, named after Isaac _____ in recognition of his work on classical mechanics.

The _____ is the unit of force derived in the SI system; it is equal to the amount of force required to accelerate a mass of one kilogram at a rate of one meter per second per second. Algebraically:

$$1\ N = 1\ \frac{kg \cdot m}{s^2}.$$

- 1 N is the force of Earth's gravity on an object with a mass of about 102 g ($1/_{9.8}$ kg) (such as a small apple.)
- On Earth's surface, a mass of 1 kg exerts a force of approximately 9.80665 N [down] (or 1 kgf.) The approximation of 1 kg corresponding to 10 N is sometimes used as a rule of thumb in everyday life and in engineering.
- The force of Earth's gravity on a human being with a mass of 70 kg is approximately 687 N.
- The dot product of force and distance is mechanical work. Thus, in SI units, a force of 1 N exerted over a distance of 1 m is 1 N·m of work. The Work-Energy Theorem states that the work done on a body is equal to the change in energy of the body. 1 N·m = 1 J (joule), the SI unit of energy.
- It is common to see forces expressed in kilonewtons or kN, where 1 kN = 1 000 N.

a. 120-cell
c. 2-3 heap

b. 1-center problem
d. Newton

47. In geometry and trigonometry, a _____ is defined as an angle between two straight intersecting lines of ninety degrees, or one-quarter of a circle.

a. Sine integral
c. Trigonometric functions

b. Trigonometry
d. Right angle

48. _____ is a branch of mathematics that deals with triangles, particularly those plane triangles in which one angle has 90 degrees. _____ deals with relationships between the sides and the angles of triangles and with the trigonometric functions, which describe those relationships.

_____ has applications in both pure mathematics and in applied mathematics, where it is essential in many branches of science and technology.

a. Law of sines
c. Trigonometric functions

b. Sine
d. Trigonometry

Chapter 8. GEOMETRY

49. In geometry and trigonometry, an _____ is the figure formed by two rays sharing a common endpoint, called the vertex of the _____. The magnitude of the _____ is the 'amount of rotation' that separates the two rays, and can be measured by considering the length of circular arc swept out when one ray is rotated about the vertex to coincide with the other. Where there is no possibility of confusion, the term '_____' is used interchangeably for both the geometric configuration itself and for its angular magnitude.
   a. A Mathematical Theory of Communication
   b. Angle
   c. A posteriori
   d. A chemical equation

50. In geometry, an _____ is a triangle in which all three sides have equal lengths. In traditional or Euclidean geometry, _____s are also equiangular; that is, all three internal angles are also equal to each other and are each 60°. They are regular polygons, and can therefore also be referred to as regular triangles.
   a. A Mathematical Theory of Communication
   b. A chemical equation
   c. Isotomic conjugate
   d. Equilateral triangle

51. In mathematics, the _____ functions are functions of an angle; they are important when studying triangles and modeling periodic phenomena, among many other applications.
   a. Coversine
   b. Law of sines
   c. Gudermannian function
   d. Trigonometric

52. The _____ of an angle is the ratio of the length of the opposite side to the length of the hypotenuse. In our case

$$\sin A = \frac{\text{opposite}}{\text{hypotenuse}} = \frac{a}{h}.$$

Note that this ratio does not depend on size of the particular right triangle chosen, as long as it contains the angle A, since all such triangles are similar.

The cosine of an angle is the ratio of the length of the adjacent side to the length of the hypotenuse.

   a. Trigonometric functions
   b. Law of sines
   c. Sine
   d. Right angle

53. In trigonometry, the _____ is a function defined as $\tan x = \sin x / \cos x$. The function is so-named because it can be defined as the length of a certain segment of a _____ (in the geometric sense) to the unit circle. In plane geometry, a line is _____ to a curve, at some point, if both line and curve pass through the point with the same direction.
   a. Tangent
   b. Projective connection
   c. Conformal geometry
   d. Hopf conjectures

54. An angle smaller than a right angle is called an _____ (less than 90 degrees).
   a. Integral geometry
   b. Euclidean geometry
   c. Acute angle
   d. Ultraparallel theorem

55. A _____ is a device for performing mathematical calculations, distinguished from a computer by having a limited problem solving ability and an interface optimized for interactive calculation rather than programming. _____s can be hardware or software, and mechanical or electronic, and are often built into devices such as PDAs or mobile phones.

Chapter 8. GEOMETRY

Modern electronic _____s are generally small, digital, and usually inexpensive.

   a. 2-3 heap
   b. 120-cell
   c. 1-center problem
   d. Calculator

56. In mathematics, the _____ of a number n is the number that, when added to n, yields zero. The _____ of n is denoted −n. For example, 7 is −7, because 7 + (−7) = 0, and the _____ of −0.3 is 0.3, because −0.3 + 0.3 = 0.
   a. Algebraic structure
   b. Associativity
   c. Additive inverse
   d. Arity

57. The Q-TIP of a geographic location is its height above a fixed reference point, often the mean sea level. _____, or geometric height, is mainly used when referring to points on the Earth's surface, while altitude or geopotential height is used for points above the surface, such as an aircraft in flight or a spacecraft in orbit.

Less commonly, _____ is measured using the center of the Earth as the reference point.

   a. Elevation
   b. A posteriori
   c. A chemical equation
   d. A Mathematical Theory of Communication

58. In mathematics, a _____ is a curve obtained by intersecting a cone with a plane. A _____ is therefore a restriction of a quadric surface to the plane. The _____s were named and studied as long ago as 200 BC, when Apollonius of Perga undertook a systematic study of their properties.
   a. Parabola
   b. Dandelin sphere
   c. Directrix
   d. Conic section

59. In mathematics, the _____ is a conic section, the intersection of a right circular conical surface and a plane parallel to a generating straight line of that surface. Given a point and a line that lie in a plane, the locus of points in that plane that are equidistant to them is a _____.

A particular case arises when the plane is tangent to the conical surface of a circle.

   a. Directrix
   b. Dandelin sphere
   c. Matrix representation of conic sections
   d. Parabola

60. In geometry, a _____ is a special kind of point, usually a corner of a polygon, polyhedron, or higher dimensional polytope. In the geometry of curves a _____ is a point of where the first derivative of curvature is zero. In graph theory, a _____ is the fundamental unit out of which graphs are formed
   a. Dini
   b. Vertex
   c. Duality
   d. Crib

61. In mathematics an _____ , a 'falling short') is a conic section, the locus of points in a plane such that the sum of the distances to two fixed points is equal to a given constant. The two fixed points are then called foci.

Another way is to define it as the path traced out by a point whose distance from a focus maintains a constant ratio less than one with its distance from a straight line not passing through the focus, called the directrix.

a. A posteriori
b. A chemical equation
c. A Mathematical Theory of Communication
d. Ellipse

62. In geometry, the _____ are a pair of special points used in describing conic sections. The four types of conic sections are the circle, parabola, ellipse, and hyperbola.
   a. Heap
   b. Foci
   c. C-35
   d. Boussinesq approximation

63. A _____ of a curve is the envelope of a family of congruent circles centered on the curve. It generalises the concept of _____ lines.

It is sometimes called the offset curve but the term 'offset' often refers also to translation.

   a. Cissoid
   b. Bifolium
   c. Cycloid
   d. Parallel

64. In geometry, the _____ is a distinctive axiom in what is now called Euclidean geometry. It states that:

If a line segment intersects two straight lines forming two interior angles on the same side that sum to less than two right angles, then the two lines, if extended indefinitely, meet on that side on which the angles sum to less than two right angles.

Euclidean geometry is the study of geometry that satisfies all of Euclid's axioms, including the _____. A geometry where the _____ cannot hold is known as a non-euclidean geometry.

   a. Cuboid
   b. Parallel postulate
   c. Circumscribed sphere
   d. Semicircle

65. In geometry, a _____ is the region in a plane bounded by a circle.

A _____ is said to be closed or open according to whether or not it contains the circle that constitutes its boundary. In Cartesian coordinates, the open _____ of center and radius R is given by the formula

$$D = \{(x,y) \in \mathbb{R}^2 : (x-a)^2 + (y-b)^2 < R^2\}$$

while the closed _____ of the same center and radius is given by

$$\overline{D} = \{(x,y) \in \mathbb{R}^2 : (x-a)^2 + (y-b)^2 \leq R^2\}.$$

The area of a closed or open _____ of radius R is πR^2.

   a. Disk
   b. Boussinesq approximation
   c. Deltoid
   d. Congruent

Chapter 8. GEOMETRY

66. _____ is a mathematical system attributed to the Greek mathematician Euclid of Alexandria. Euclid's Elements is the earliest known systematic discussion of geometry. It has been one of the most influential books in history, as much for its method as for its mathematical content.
   a. Infinitely near point
   b. Equidimensional
   c. Analytic geometry
   d. Euclidean geometry

67. A _____ of a sphere is a circle that runs along the surface of that sphere so as to cut it into two equal halves. The _____ therefore has both the same circumference and the same center as the sphere. It is the largest circle that can be drawn on a given sphere.
   a. Perimeter
   b. Cathetus
   c. Line segment
   d. Great circle

68. The existence and properties of _____ are the basis of Euclid's parallel postulate. _____ are two lines on the same plane that do not intersect even assuming that lines extend to infinity in either direction.
   a. Vertical translation
   b. Spidron
   c. Square wheel
   d. Parallel lines

69. In mathematics, a _____ is, informally, an infinitely vast and infinitely thin sheet. _____s may be thought of as objects in some higher dimensional space, or they may be considered without any outside space, as in the setting of Euclidean geometry
   a. Bandwidth
   b. Blocking
   c. Group
   d. Plane

70. _____ is the branch of differential geometry that studies Riemannian manifolds, smooth manifolds with a Riemannian metric. This gives in particular local notions of angle, length of curves, surface area, and volume. From those some other global quantities can be derived by integrating local contributions.
   a. Hopf-Rinow theorem
   b. Hodge theory
   c. Nash embedding theorem
   d. Riemannian geometry

71. Geometric modeing is the construction or use of _____. Geometric models are used in computer graphics, computer-aided design and manufacturing, and many applied fields such as medical image processing.

   _____ can be built for objects of any dimension in any geometric space.

   a. Geometric models
   b. Continuous symmetry
   c. Control theory
   d. Control limits

72. In mathematics, the _____ is an approach to finding a particular solution to certain inhomogeneous ordinary differential equations and recurrence relations. It is closely related to the annihilator method, but instead of using a particular kind of differential operator in order to find the best possible form of the particular solution, a 'guess' is made as to the appropriate form, which is then tested by differentiating the resulting equation. In this sense, the _____ is less formal but more intuitive than the annihilator method.
   a. Differential algebraic equations
   b. Linear differential equation
   c. Method of undetermined coefficients
   d. Phase line

73. In ecology, predation describes a biological interaction where a _____ (an organism that is hunting) feeds on its prey, the organism that is attacked. _____s may or may not kill their prey prior to feeding on them, but the act of predation always results in the death of the prey. The other main category of consumption is detritivory, the consumption of dead organic material (detritus.)

a. 120-cell
b. 1-center problem
c. Prey
d. Predator

74. In linear algebra, two n-by-n matrices A and B over the field K are called _____ if there exists an invertible n-by-n matrix P over K such that

$$P^{-1}AP = B.$$

One of the meanings of the term similarity transformation is such a transformation of a matrix A into a matrix B.

Similarity is an equivalence relation on the space of square matrices.

_____ matrices share many properties:

- rank
- determinant
- trace
- eigenvalues
- characteristic polynomial
- minimal polynomial
- elementary divisors

There are two reasons for these facts:

- two _____ matrices can be thought of as describing the same linear map, but with respect to different bases
- the map $X \mapsto P^{-1}XP$ is an automorphism of the associative algebra of all n-by-n matrices, as the one-object case of the above category of all matrices.

Because of this, for a given matrix A, one is interested in finding a simple 'normal form' B which is _____ to A -- the study of A then reduces to the study of the simpler matrix B.

a. Blinding
b. Coherence
c. Dense
d. Similar

75. In mathematics, _____ describes hyperbolic and elliptic geometry, which are contrasted with Euclidean geometry. The essential difference between Euclidean and _____ is the nature of parallel lines. Euclid's fifth postulate, the parallel postulate, is equivalent to Playfair's postulate, which states that, within a two-dimensional plane, for any given line l and a point A, which is not on l, there is exactly one line through A that does not intersect l.

Chapter 8. GEOMETRY

a. Nash function
c. Non-Euclidean geometry
b. Tropical geometry
d. Brascamp-Lieb inequality

76. A _____ is a structured activity, usually undertaken for enjoyment and sometimes also used as an educational tool. _____s are distinct from work, which is usually carried out for remuneration, and from art, which is more concerned with the expression of ideas. However, the distinction is not clear-cut, and many _____s are also considered to be work (such as professional players of spectator sports/_____s) or art (such as jigsaw puzzles or _____s involving an artistic layout such as Mah-jongg solitaire.)

a. Game
c. 2-3 heap
b. 1-center problem
d. 120-cell

77. In mathematics, the _____ is a fractal curve. It is the universal curve, in that it has topological dimension one, and any other curve is homeomorphic to some subset of it. It is sometimes called the Menger-Sierpinski sponge or the Sierpinski sponge.

a. Minkowski-Bouligand dimension
c. Mandelbrot set
b. Gravity set
d. Menger sponge

78. In mathematics, a self-similar object is exactly or approximately similar to a part of itself. Many objects in the real world, such as coastlines, are statistically self-similar: parts of them show the same statistical properties at many scales. _____ is a typical property of fractals.

a. Cantor function
c. Gravity set
b. Hausdorff dimension
d. Self-similarity

79. A _____ is a software program that facilitates symbolic mathematics. The core functionality of a CAS is manipulation of mathematical expressions in symbolic form.

The symbolic manipulations supported typically include

- simplification to the smallest possible expression or some standard form, including automatic simplification with assumptions and simplification with constraints
- substitution of symbolic, functors or numeric values for expressions
- change of form of expressions: expanding products and powers, partial and full factorization, rewriting as partial fractions, constraint satisfaction, rewriting trigonometric functions as exponentials, etc.
- partial and total differentiation
- symbolic constrained and unconstrained global optimization
- solution of linear and some non-linear equations over various domains
- solution of some differential and difference equations
- taking some limits
- some indefinite and definite integration, including multidimensional integrals
- integral transforms
- arbitrary-precision numeric operations
- Series operations such as expansion, summation and products
- matrix operations including products, inverses, etc.
- display of mathematical expressions in two-dimensional mathematical form, often using typesetting systems similar to TeX
- add-ons for use in applied mathematics such as physics packages for physical computation
- plotting graphs and parametric plots of functions in two and three dimensions, and animating them
- APIs for linking it on an external program such as a database, or using in a programming language to use the _____
- drawing charts and diagrams
- string manipulation such as matching and searching
- statistical computation
- Theorem proving and verification
- graphic production and editing such as CGI and signal processing as image processing
- sound synthesis

Many also include a programming language, allowing users to implement their own algorithms.

Some _____s focus on a specific area of application; these are typically developed in academia and are free.

a. Computer algebra system
c. 1-center problem
b. 2-3 heap
d. 120-cell

80. The _____ is a plane fractal first described by Wacław Sierpiński in 1916. The carpet is a generalization of the Cantor set to two dimensions. Sierpiński demonstrated that this fractal is a universal curve, in that any possible one-dimensional graph, projected onto the two-dimensional plane, is homeomorphic to a subset of the _____.

a. Hausdorff dimension
c. Fractal transform
b. Multifractal system
d. Sierpinski carpet

Chapter 9. GRAPH THEORY

1. In mathematics and computer science, _____ is the study of graphs: mathematical structures used to model pairwise relations between objects from a certain collection. A 'graph' in this context refers to a collection of vertices or 'nodes' and a collection of edges that connect pairs of vertices. A graph may be undirected, meaning that there is no distinction between the two vertices associated with each edge, or its edges may be directed from one vertex to another; see graph for more detailed definitions and for other variations in the types of graphs that are commonly considered.
   - a. Pooling design
   - b. Partial equivalence relation
   - c. Discrete mathematics
   - d. Graph theory

2. The word _____ has many distinct meanings in different fields of knowledge, depending on their methodologies and the context of discussion. Broadly speaking we can say that a _____ is some kind of belief or claim that (supposedly) explains, asserts, or consolidates some class of claims. Additionally, in contrast with a theorem the statement of the _____ is generally accepted only in some tentative fashion as opposed to regarding it as having been conclusively established.
   - a. Per mil
   - b. Transport of structure
   - c. Defined
   - d. Theory

3. In graph theory, a _____ is an edge that connects a vertex to itself. A simple graph contains no _____s.

Depending on the context, a graph or a multigraph may be defined so as to either allow or disallow the presence of _____s:

- Where graphs are defined so as to allow _____s and multiple edges, a graph without _____s is often called a multigraph.
- Where graphs are defined so as to disallow _____s and multiple edges, a multigraph or a pseudograph is often defined to mean a 'graph' which can have _____s and multiple edges.

For an undirected graph, the degree of a vertex is equal to the number of adjacent vertices.

A special case is a _____, which adds two to the degree.

   - a. Commensurable
   - b. FISH
   - c. Duality
   - d. Loop

4. In geometry, a _____ is a special kind of point, usually a corner of a polygon, polyhedron, or higher dimensional polytope. In the geometry of curves a _____ is a point of where the first derivative of curvature is zero. In graph theory, a _____ is the fundamental unit out of which graphs are formed
   - a. Dini
   - b. Duality
   - c. Crib
   - d. Vertex

5. _____ is a quantity expressing the two-dimensional size of a defined part of a surface, typically a region bounded by a closed curve. The term surface _____ refers to the total _____ of the exposed surface of a 3-dimensional solid, such as the sum of the _____s of the exposed sides of a polyhedron. _____ is an important invariant in the differential geometry of surfaces.
   - a. A chemical equation
   - b. Area
   - c. A Mathematical Theory of Communication
   - d. A posteriori

6. _____ is an adjective meaning contiguous, adjoining or abutting.

Chapter 9. GRAPH THEORY

In geometry, _____ is when sides meet to make an angle.

In trigonometry the _____ side of a right angled triangle is the cathetus next to the angle in question.

a. Adjacent
b. Ordered geometry
c. Ambient space
d. Affine geometry

7. In graph theory, an _____ of a vertex v in a graph is a vertex that is connected to v by an edge. The neighbourhood of a vertex v in a graph G is the induced subgraph of G consisting of all vertices adjacent to v and all edges connecting two such vertices. For example, the image shows a graph of 6 vertices and 7 edges.

a. Adjacent vertex
b. Articulation point
c. Independent set
d. Induced path

8. In mathematics and computer science, _____ (also base-16, hexa or base, of 16. It uses sixteen distinct symbols, most often the symbols 0-9 to represent values zero to nine, and A, B, C, D, E, F (or a through f) to represent values ten to fifteen.

Its primary use is as a human friendly representation of binary coded values, so it is often used in digital electronics and computer engineering.

a. Hexadecimal
b. Radix
c. Factoradic
d. Tetradecimal

9. In mathematics, a _____ is a statement that can be proved on the basis of explicitly stated or previously agreed assumptions.

a. Theorem
b. Disjunction introduction
c. Boolean function
d. Logical value

10. In mathematics, computing, linguistics and related subjects, an _____ is a sequence of finite instructions, often used for calculation and data processing. It is formally a type of effective method in which a list of well-defined instructions for completing a task will, when given an initial state, proceed through a well-defined series of successive states, eventually terminating in an end-state. The transition from one state to the next is not necessarily deterministic; some _____s, known as probabilistic _____s, incorporate randomness.

a. In-place algorithm
b. Out-of-core
c. Algorithm
d. Approximate counting algorithm

11. In graph theory, an _____ is a path in a graph which visits each edge exactly once. Similarly, an Eulerian circuit is an _____ which starts and ends on the same vertex. They were first discussed by Leonhard Euler while solving the famous Seven Bridges of Königsberg problem in 1736.

a. Isomorphism of graphs
b. Independent set
c. Eulerian path
d. Adjacent vertex

12. The _____ program is a directory search utility on Unix-like platforms. It searches through one or more directory trees of a filesystem, locating files based on some user-specified criteria. By default, _____ returns all files below the current working directory.

Chapter 9. GRAPH THEORY

a. 2-3 heap
c. 1-center problem
b. Find
d. 120-cell

13. A _____ or digraph is a pair G= of:

- a set V, whose elements are called vertices or nodes,
- a set A of ordered pairs of vertices, called arcs, directed edges, or arrows

It differs from an ordinary, or undirected graph in that the latter one is defined in terms of edges, which are unordered pairs of vertices.

Sometimes a digraph is called a simple digraph to distinguish from the case of directed multigraph, in which the arcs constitute a multiset, rather than a set, of ordered pairs of vertices. Also, in a simple digraph loops. On the other hand, some texts allow both loops and multiple arcs in a digraph.

a. 2-3 heap
c. 1-center problem
b. Directed graph
d. 120-cell

14. In the physical sciences, _____ is a measurement of the gravitational force acting on an object. Near the surface of the Earth, the acceleration due to gravity is approximately constant; this means that an object's _____ is roughly proportional to its mass.

In commerce and in many other applications, _____ means the same as mass as that term is used in physics.

a. 120-cell
c. 1-center problem
b. 2-3 heap
d. Weight

15. In mathematics, _____ and undefined are used to explain whether or not expressions have meaningful, sensible, and unambiguous values. Not all branches of mathematics come to the same conclusion.

The following expressions are undefined in all contexts, but remarks in the analysis section may apply.

a. Plugging in
c. LHS
b. Defined
d. Toy model

16. In the mathematical field of graph theory, a _____ T of a connected, undirected graph G is a tree composed of all the vertices and some of the edges of G. Informally, a _____ of G is a selection of edges of G that form a tree spanning every vertex. That is, every vertex lies in the tree, but no cycles are formed.

a. Chord
c. Germ
b. Lattice
d. Spanning tree

17. In set theory, a _____ is a partially ordered set such that for each $t \in T$, the set $\{s \in T : s < t\}$ is well-ordered by the relation <. For each $t \in T$, the order type of $\{s \in T : s < t\}$ is called the height of t. The height of T itself is the least ordinal greater than the height of each element of T.

Chapter 9. GRAPH THEORY

a. Tree
c. Definable numbers
b. Transitive reduction
d. Set-theoretic topology

18. _____ is a book by Matt Curtin about cryptography.

In this book, the author accounts his involvement in the DESCHALL Project, mobilizing thousands of personal computers in 1997 in order to meet the challenge to crack a single message encrypted with DES.

This was and remains one of the largest collaborations of any kind on a single project in history.

a. Brute force
c. Development
b. Blind
d. Congruent

19. In mathematical analysis, a metric space M is said to be _____ (or Cauchy) if every Cauchy sequence of points in M has a limit that is also in M or alternatively if every Cauchy sequence in M converges in M.

Intuitively, a space is _____ if there are no 'points missing' from it (inside or at the boundary.) For instance, the set of rational numbers is not _____, because $\sqrt{2}$ is 'missing' from it, even though one can construct a Cauchy sequence of rational numbers that converges to it.

a. 120-cell
c. 1-center problem
b. 2-3 heap
d. Complete

20. In the mathematical field of graph theory, a _____ is a simple graph in which every pair of distinct vertices is connected by an edge. The _____ on n vertices has n vertices and n edges, and is denoted by K_n. It is a regular graph of degree n − 1.

a. 1-center problem
c. Wheel graph
b. 120-cell
d. Complete graph

21. A _____ is a group of interconnected computers. Networks may be classified according to a wide variety of characteristics

a. Computer network
c. Flooding algorithm
b. Leader election
d. HTTP compression

22. In graph theory, a _____ is a digraph with weighted edges. These _____s have become an especially useful concept in analysing the interaction between biology and mathematics. Using _____s of all types; various applications based on the creativity of the mathematician along with their environment can be evaluated in all sorts of manners.

a. Colossus
c. Chord
b. Copula
d. Network

23. In linear algebra, two n-by-n matrices A and B over the field K are called _____ if there exists an invertible n-by-n matrix P over K such that

Chapter 9. GRAPH THEORY

$$P^{-1}AP = B.$$

One of the meanings of the term similarity transformation is such a transformation of a matrix A into a matrix B.

Similarity is an equivalence relation on the space of square matrices.

_____ matrices share many properties:

- rank
- determinant
- trace
- eigenvalues
- characteristic polynomial
- minimal polynomial
- elementary divisors

There are two reasons for these facts:

- two _____ matrices can be thought of as describing the same linear map, but with respect to different bases
- the map X ⟼ P⁻¹XP is an automorphism of the associative algebra of all n-by-n matrices, as the one-object case of the above category of all matrices.

Because of this, for a given matrix A, one is interested in finding a simple 'normal form' B which is _____ to A -- the study of A then reduces to the study of the simpler matrix B.

a. Dense
c. Similar
b. Coherence
d. Blinding

24. In geometry and trigonometry, an _____ is the figure formed by two rays sharing a common endpoint, called the vertex of the _____. The magnitude of the _____ is the 'amount of rotation' that separates the two rays, and can be measured by considering the length of circular arc swept out when one ray is rotated about the vertex to coincide with the other. Where there is no possibility of confusion, the term '_____' is used interchangeably for both the geometric configuration itself and for its angular magnitude.

a. Angle
c. A posteriori
b. A Mathematical Theory of Communication
d. A chemical equation

25. A _____ is one of the basic shapes of geometry: a polygon with three corners or vertices and three sides or edges which are line segments. A _____ with vertices A, B, and C is denoted ABC.

In Euclidean geometry any three non-collinear points determine a unique _____ and a unique plane.

84 Chapter 9. GRAPH THEORY

   a. Fuhrmann circle
   c. Kepler triangle
   b. 1-center problem
   d. Triangle

26. In mathematics and statistics, the _____ of a list of numbers is the sum of all of the list divided by the number of items in the list. If the list is a statistical population, then the mean of that population is called a population mean. If the list is a statistical sample, we call the resulting statistic a sample mean.
   a. Unsolved problems in statistics
   c. Interval estimation
   b. Analysis of variance
   d. Arithmetic mean

27. In statistics, _____ has two related meanings:

   - the arithmetic _____.
   - the expected value of a random variable, which is also called the population _____.

It is sometimes stated that the '_____' _____s average. This is incorrect if '_____' is taken in the specific sense of 'arithmetic _____' as there are different types of averages: the _____, median, and mode. For instance, average house prices almost always use the median value for the average.

For a real-valued random variable X, the _____ is the expectation of X.

   a. Statistical population
   c. Mean
   b. Proportional hazards model
   d. Probability

28. In commutative algebra, the term _____ refers to several related functors on topological rings and modules. _____ is similar to localization, and together they are among the most basic tools in analysing commutative rings. Complete commutative rings have simpler structure than the general ones, in large part, due to Hensel's lemma.
   a. Colossus
   c. Completion
   b. Battle of the Sexes
   d. Decimal system

29. A _____ is a type of bar chart that illustrates a project schedule. _____s illustrate the start and finish dates of the terminal elements and summary elements of a project. Terminal elements and summary elements comprise the work breakdown structure of the project.
   a. Gantt chart
   c. 2-3 heap
   b. 1-center problem
   d. 120-cell

30. _____ Any process by which a specified characteristic usually amplitude of the output of a device is prevented from exceeding a predetermined value.
   a. Notation
   c. Logical equivalence
   b. Limiting
   d. Parametric continuity

31. A _____ of a curve is the envelope of a family of congruent circles centered on the curve. It generalises the concept of _____ lines.

It is sometimes called the offset curve but the term 'offset' often refers also to translation.

a. Cycloid
b. Cissoid
c. Parallel
d. Bifolium

32. _____ is an important tool for manufacturing and engineering, where it can have a major impact on the productivity of a process. In manufacturing, the purpose of _____ is to minimize the production time and costs, by telling a production facility what to make, when, with which staff, and on which equipment. Production _____ aims to maximize the efficiency of the operation and reduce costs.

a. Scheduling
b. Crib
c. Critical point
d. Boolean algebra

33. In graph theory, a _____ in a graph is a sequence of vertices such that from each of its vertices there is an edge to the next vertex in the sequence. The first vertex is called the start vertex and the last vertex is called the end vertex. Both of them are called end or terminal vertices of the _____.

a. Class
b. Blinding
c. Deltoid
d. Path

34. In computational complexity theory, an algorithm is said to take _____ if the asymptotic upper bound for the time it requires is proportional to the size of the input, which is usually denoted n.

Informally spoken, the running time increases linearly with the size of the input. For example, a procedure that adds up all elements of a list requires time proportional to the length of the list.

a. Truth table reduction
b. Constructible function
c. Linear time
d. Time-constructible function

Chapter 10. EXPONENTIAL AND LOGARITHMIC FUNCTIONS

1. In mathematics and computer science, _____ (also base-16, hexa or base, of 16. It uses sixteen distinct symbols, most often the symbols 0-9 to represent values zero to nine, and A, B, C, D, E, F (or a through f) to represent values ten to fifteen.

   Its primary use is as a human friendly representation of binary coded values, so it is often used in digital electronics and computer engineering.

   a. Radix
   b. Factoradic
   c. Tetradecimal
   d. Hexadecimal

2. _____ and independent variables refer to values that change in relationship to each other. The _____ are those that are observed to change in response to the independent variables. The independent variables are those that are deliberately manipulated to invoke a change in the _____.

   a. Steiner system
   b. Dependent variables
   c. Round robin test
   d. Yates analysis

3. Dependent variables and _____ refer to values that change in relationship to each other. The dependent variables are those that are observed to change in response to the _____. The _____ are those that are deliberately manipulated to invoke a change in the dependent variables.

   a. One-factor-at-a-time method
   b. Operational confound
   c. Experimental design diagram
   d. Independent variables

4. A _____ is a device for performing mathematical calculations, distinguished from a computer by having a limited problem solving ability and an interface optimized for interactive calculation rather than programming. _____s can be hardware or software, and mechanical or electronic, and are often built into devices such as PDAs or mobile phones.

   Modern electronic _____s are generally small, digital, and usually inexpensive.

   a. 1-center problem
   b. 2-3 heap
   c. 120-cell
   d. Calculator

5. In mathematics, _____ and undefined are used to explain whether or not expressions have meaningful, sensible, and unambiguous values. Not all branches of mathematics come to the same conclusion.

   The following expressions are undefined in all contexts, but remarks in the analysis section may apply.

   a. LHS
   b. Toy model
   c. Defined
   d. Plugging in

6. The _____ is a function in mathematics. The application of this function to a value x is written as ex. Equivalently, this can be written in the form e^x, where e is a mathematical constant, the base of the natural logarithm, which equals approximately 2.718281828, and is also known as Euler's number.

   a. Area hyperbolic functions
   b. Exponential function
   c. A chemical equation
   d. A Mathematical Theory of Communication

Chapter 10. EXPONENTIAL AND LOGARITHMIC FUNCTIONS

7. The mathematical concept of a _____ expresses the intuitive idea of deterministic dependence between two quantities, one of which is viewed as primary and the other as secondary. A _____ then is a way to associate a unique output for each input of a specified type, for example, a real number or an element of a given set.
   - a. Going up
   - b. Grill
   - c. Coherent
   - d. Function

8. In linear algebra, _____ is a version of Gaussian elimination that puts zeros both above and below each pivot element as it goes from the top row of the given matrix to the bottom. In other words, _____ brings a matrix to reduced row echelon form, whereas Gaussian elimination takes it only as far as row echelon form. Every matrix has a reduced row echelon form, and this algorithm is guaranteed to produce it.
   - a. Lax equivalence theorem
   - b. Conservation form
   - c. Spheroidal wave functions
   - d. Gauss-Jordan elimination

9. In mathematics, a _____ is a number which can be expressed as a ratio of two integers. Non-integer _____s are usually written as the vulgar fraction $\frac{a}{b}$, where b is not zero. a is called the numerator, and b the denominator.
   - a. Rational number
   - b. Minkowski distance
   - c. Tally marks
   - d. Pre-algebra

10. An angle smaller than a right angle is called an _____ (less than 90 degrees).
    - a. Integral geometry
    - b. Acute angle
    - c. Euclidean geometry
    - d. Ultraparallel theorem

11. In geometry and trigonometry, an _____ is the figure formed by two rays sharing a common endpoint, called the vertex of the _____. The magnitude of the _____ is the 'amount of rotation' that separates the two rays, and can be measured by considering the length of circular arc swept out when one ray is rotated about the vertex to coincide with the other. Where there is no possibility of confusion, the term '_____' is used interchangeably for both the geometric configuration itself and for its angular magnitude.
    - a. A Mathematical Theory of Communication
    - b. A posteriori
    - c. Angle
    - d. A chemical equation

12. In mathematics, the _____ of a number to a given base is the power or exponent to which the base must be raised in order to produce the number.

    For example, the _____ of 1000 to the base 10 is 3, because 3 is how many 10s one must multiply to get 1000: thus 10 × 10 × 10 = 1000; the base-2 _____ of 32 is 5 because 5 is how many 2s one must multiply to get 32: thus 2 × 2 × 2 × 2 × 2 = 32. In the language of exponents: 10^3 = 1000, so $\log_{10} 1000 = 3$, and $2^5 = 32$, so $\log_2 32 = 5$.

    - a. 1-center problem
    - b. 120-cell
    - c. 2-3 heap
    - d. Logarithm

13. A _____ is one of the basic shapes of geometry: a polygon with three corners or vertices and three sides or edges which are line segments. A _____ with vertices A, B, and C is denoted ABC.

Chapter 10. EXPONENTIAL AND LOGARITHMIC FUNCTIONS

In Euclidean geometry any three non-collinear points determine a unique _____ and a unique plane.

a. Triangle
b. 1-center problem
c. Kepler triangle
d. Fuhrmann circle

14. The _____ is the logarithm with base 10. It is also known as the decadic logarithm, named after its base. It is indicated by $\log_{10}$

a. Logarithmic growth
b. 1-center problem
c. Common logarithm
d. Natural logarithm

15. The function $\log_b(x)$ depends on both b and x, but the term _____ (or logarithmic function) in standard usage refers to a function of the form $\log_b(x)$ in which the base b is fixed and so the only argument is x. Thus there is one _____ for each value of the base b (which must be positive and must differ from 1.) Viewed in this way, the base-b _____ is the inverse function of the exponential function b^x.

a. 2-3 heap
b. Logarithm function
c. 1-center problem
d. 120-cell

16. The _____, formerly known as the hyperbolic logarithm, is the logarithm to the base e, where e is an irrational constant approximately equal to 2.718 281 828. It is also sometimes referred to as the Napierian logarithm, although the original meaning of this term is slightly different. In simple terms, the _____ of a number x is the power to which e would have to be raised to equal x -- for example the natural log of e itself is 1 because e^1 = e, while the _____ of 1 would be 0, since e^0 = 1.

a. Logarithmic identities
b. 1-center problem
c. Logarithmic growth
d. Natural logarithm

17. In mathematics, the _____ of a number n is the number that, when added to n, yields zero. The _____ of n is denoted −n. For example, 7 is −7, because 7 + (−7) = 0, and the _____ of −0.3 is 0.3, because −0.3 + 0.3 = 0.

a. Algebraic structure
b. Associativity
c. Arity
d. Additive inverse

18. The _____ is a mathematical curve and one of the earliest fractal curves to have been described. It appeared in a 1904 paper entitled "On a continuous curve without tangents constructible from elementary geometry" by the Swedish mathematician Helge von Koch.

a. 2-3 heap
b. 120-cell
c. Koch snowflake
d. 1-center problem

19. A _____ is generally 'a rough or fragmented geometric shape that can be split into parts, each of which is a reduced-size copy of the whole,' a property called self-similarity. The term was coined by Benoît Mandelbrot in 1975 and was derived from the Latin fractus meaning 'broken' or 'fractured.' A mathematical _____ is based on an equation that undergoes iteration, a form of feedback based on recursion.

Chapter 10. EXPONENTIAL AND LOGARITHMIC FUNCTIONS   89

A _____ often has the following features:

- It has a fine structure at arbitrarily small scales.
- It is too irregular to be easily described in traditional Euclidean geometric language.
- It is self-similar.
- It has a Hausdorff dimension which is greater than its topological dimension.
- It has a simple and recursive definition.

Because they appear similar at all levels of magnification, _____s are often considered to be infinitely complex. Natural objects that approximate _____s to a degree include clouds, mountain ranges, lightning bolts, coastlines, and snow flakes.

a. Fractal
b. Logical disjunction
c. Zero-point energy
d. Cube

20. _____ is a part of mathematics concerned with questions of size, shape, and relative position of figures and with properties of space. _____ is one of the oldest sciences. Initially a body of practical knowledge concerning lengths, areas, and volumes, in the third century BC _____ was put into an axiomatic form by Euclid, whose treatment--Euclidean _____--set a standard for many centuries to follow.

a. 120-cell
b. 2-3 heap
c. 1-center problem
d. Geometry

21. _____ occurs when the growth rate of a mathematical function is proportional to the function's current value. In the case of a discrete domain of definition with equal intervals it is also called geometric growth or geometric decay.

With _____ of a positive value its rate of increase steadily increases, or in the case of exponential decay, its rate of decrease steadily decreases.

a. A posteriori
b. A chemical equation
c. A Mathematical Theory of Communication
d. Exponential growth

22. A _____ is an abstract model that uses mathematical language to describe the behavior of a system. Eykhoff defined a _____ as 'a representation of the essential aspects of an existing system which presents knowledge of that system in usable form'.

a. Mathematical model
b. Total least squares
c. Rata Die
d. Metaheuristic

23. _____ is the concept of adding accumulated interest back to the principal, so that interest is earned on interest from that moment on. The act of declaring interest to be principal is called compounding. A loan, for example, may have its interest compounded every month: in this case, a loan with $100 principal and 1% interest per month would have a balance of $101 at the end of the first month.

a. Net interest margin
b. Retained interest
c. Net interest margin securities
d. Compound interest

24. _____ is a fee, paid on borrowed capital. Assets lent include money, shares, consumer goods through hire purchase, major assets such as aircraft, and even entire factories in finance lease arrangements. The _____ is calculated upon the value of the assets in the same manner as upon money.
   - a. A Mathematical Theory of Communication
   - b. Interest sensitivity gap
   - c. Interest expense
   - d. Interest

25. A quantity is said to be subject to _____ if it decreases at a rate proportional to its value. Symbolically, this can be expressed as the following differential equation, where N is the quantity and λ is a positive number called the decay constant.

$$\frac{dN}{dt} = -\lambda N.$$

The solution to this equation is:

$$N(t) = N_0 e^{-\lambda t}.$$

Here is the quantity at time t, and N_0 = N is the quantity, at time t = 0.

   - a. Exponential decay
   - b. Exponential integral
   - c. Exponentiating by squaring
   - d. Exponential formula

26. _____ is the process in which an unstable atomic nucleus loses energy by emitting ionizing particles and radiation. This decay, or loss of energy, results in an atom of one type, called the parent nuclide transforming to an atom of a different type, called the daughter nuclide. For example: a carbon-14 atom emits radiation and transforms to a nitrogen-14 atom.
   - a. 1-center problem
   - b. 120-cell
   - c. Half-life
   - d. Radioactive decay

27. _____, or carbon dating, is a radiometric dating method that uses the naturally occurring radioisotope carbon-14 (^{14}C) to determine the age of carbonaceous materials up to about 60,000 years. Raw, i.e. uncalibrated, radiocarbon ages are usually reported in radiocarbon years 'Before Present' (BP), 'Present' being defined as AD 1950. Such raw ages can be calibrated to give calendar dates.
   - a. Radiocarbon dating
   - b. 120-cell
   - c. 2-3 heap
   - d. 1-center problem

28. The _____ of a quantity whose value decreases with time is the interval required for the quantity to decay to half of its initial value. The concept originated in describing how long it takes atoms to undergo radioactive decay, but also applies in a wide variety of other situations.

The term '_____' dates to 1907.

   - a. Radioactive decay
   - b. 120-cell
   - c. Half-life
   - d. 1-center problem

Chapter 10. EXPONENTIAL AND LOGARITHMIC FUNCTIONS

29. In mathematics, an _____, or central tendency of a data set refers to a measure of the 'middle' or 'expected' value of the data set. There are many different descriptive statistics that can be chosen as a measurement of the central tendency of the data items.

An _____ is a single value that is meant to typify a list of values.

   a. A posteriori
   c. A chemical equation
   b. A Mathematical Theory of Communication
   d. Average

30.

A _____ is a scale of measurement that uses the logarithm of a physical quantity instead of the quantity itself.

Presentation of data on a _____ can be helpful when the data covers a large range of values - the logarithm reduces this to a more manageable range. Some of our senses operate in a logarithmic fashion, which makes _____s for these input quantities especially appropriate.

   a. Mel scale
   c. 120-cell
   b. Logarithmic scale
   d. 1-center problem

31. In mathematics the concept of a _____ generalizes notions such as 'length', 'area', and 'volume'. Informally, given some base set, a '_____' is any consistent assignment of 'sizes' to the subsets of the base set. Depending on the application, the 'size' of a subset may be interpreted as its physical size, the amount of something that lies within the subset, or the probability that some random process will yield a result within the subset.

   a. Cusp
   c. Lattice
   b. Congruent
   d. Measure

32. _____ is the magnitude of change in the oscillating variable, with each oscillation, within an oscillating system. For instance, sound waves are oscillations in atmospheric pressure and their _____s are proportional to the change in pressure during one oscillation. If the variable undergoes regular oscillations, and a graph of the system is drawn with the oscillating variable as the vertical axis and time as the horizontal axis, the _____ is visually represented by the vertical distance between the extrema of the curve.

   a. Amplitude
   c. Areal velocity
   b. Angular frequency
   d. Angular velocity

33. Seismometers are instruments that measure and record motions of the ground, including those of seismic waves generated by earthquakes, nuclear explosions, and other seismic sources. Records of seismic waves allow seismologists to map the interior of the Earth, and locate and measure the size of these different sources. _____ is another Greek term from seismós and γρÎ¬φω, gráphÃ , to draw.

   a. 120-cell
   c. 1-center problem
   b. 2-3 heap
   d. Seismograph

Chapter 10. EXPONENTIAL AND LOGARITHMIC FUNCTIONS

34. _____ is a quantity expressing the two-dimensional size of a defined part of a surface, typically a region bounded by a closed curve. The term surface _____ refers to the total _____ of the exposed surface of a 3-dimensional solid, such as the sum of the _____s of the exposed sides of a polyhedron. _____ is an important invariant in the differential geometry of surfaces.

   a. A posteriori
   b. A chemical equation
   c. A Mathematical Theory of Communication
   d. Area

35. In mathematics and in the sciences, a _____ (plural: _____e, formulæ or _____s) is a concise way of expressing information symbolically (as in a mathematical or chemical _____), or a general relationship between quantities. One of many famous _____e is Albert Einstein's E = mc² (see special relativity

In mathematics, a _____ is a key to solve an equation with variables. For example, the problem of determining the volume of a sphere is one that requires a significant amount of integral calculus to solve.

   a. 1-center problem
   b. 120-cell
   c. 2-3 heap
   d. Formula

36. In signal processing, the _____ E_s of a continuous-time signal x

$$E_s \;=\; \langle x(t), x(t) \rangle \;=\; \int_{-\infty}^{\infty} |x(t)|^2 dt$$

_____ in this context is not, strictly speaking, the same as the conventional notion of _____ in physics and the other sciences. The two concepts are, however, closely related, and it is possible to convert from one to the other:

$$E = \frac{E_s}{Z} = \frac{1}{Z}\int_{-\infty}^{\infty} |x(t)|^2 dt$$

where Z represents the magnitude, in appropriate units of measure, of the load driven by the signal.

For example, if x

   a. Audio signal processing
   b. Emphasis
   c. Essential bandwidth
   d. Energy

Chapter 11. MATRICES AND MARKOV CHAINS

1. In mathematics, a _____, named after Andrey Markov, is a stochastic process with the Markov property. Having the Markov property means that, given the present state, future states are independent of the past states. In other words, the description of the present state fully captures all the information that could influence the future evolution of the process. Future states will be reached through a probabilistic process instead of a deterministic one.
   a. Markov chain
   b. Possibility theory
   c. Law of Truly Large Numbers
   d. Variance-to-mean ratio

2. In mathematics, an _____ or member of a set is any one of the distinct objects that make up that set.

   Writing A = {1,2,3,4}, means that the _____s of the set A are the numbers 1, 2, 3 and 4. Groups of _____s of A, for example {1,2}, are subsets of A.

   a. Order
   b. Element
   c. Ideal
   d. Universal code

3. _____ is a branch of mathematics which focuses on the study of matrices. Initially a sub-branch of linear algebra, it has grown to cover subjects related to graph theory, algebra, combinatorics, and statistics as well.

   The term matrix was first coined in 1848 by J.J. Sylvester as a name of an array of numbers.

   a. Pairing
   b. Segre classification
   c. Semi-simple operators
   d. Matrix theory

4. In linear algebra, a row vector or _____ is a 1 × n matrix, that is, a matrix consisting of a single row:

$$\mathbf{x} = \begin{bmatrix} x_1 & x_2 & \ldots & x_m \end{bmatrix}.$$

The transpose of a row vector is a column vector:

$$\begin{bmatrix} x_1 \\ x_2 \\ \vdots \\ x_m \end{bmatrix} = \begin{bmatrix} x_1 & x_2 & \ldots & x_m \end{bmatrix}^\mathrm{T}.$$

The set of all row vectors forms a vector space which is the dual space to the set of all column vectors.

Row vectors are sometimes written using the following non-standard notation:

$$\mathbf{x} = \begin{bmatrix} x_1, x_2, \ldots, x_m \end{bmatrix}.$$

- Matrix multiplication involves the action of multiplying each row vector of one matrix by each column vector of another matrix.

- The dot product of two vectors a and b is equivalent to multiplying the row vector representation of a by the column vector representation of b:

$$\mathbf{a} \cdot \mathbf{b} = \begin{bmatrix} a_1 & a_2 & a_3 \end{bmatrix} \begin{bmatrix} b_1 \\ b_2 \\ b_3 \end{bmatrix}.$$

a. Woodbury matrix identity
c. Gram-Schmidt process
b. Dual vector space
d. Row matrix

5. In mathematics, _____ is a property that a binary operation can have. It means that, within an expression containing two or more of the same associative operators in a row, the order that the operations are performed does not matter as long as the sequence of the operands is not changed. That is, rearranging the parentheses in such an expression will not change its value.

a. Idempotence
c. Unital
b. Algebraically closed
d. Associativity

6. In mathematics, _____ and undefined are used to explain whether or not expressions have meaningful, sensible, and unambiguous values. Not all branches of mathematics come to the same conclusion.

The following expressions are undefined in all contexts, but remarks in the analysis section may apply.

a. Defined
c. LHS
b. Plugging in
d. Toy model

7. In mathematics, a _____ is a rectangular table of elements, which may be numbers or, more generally, any abstract quantities that can be added and multiplied. Matrices are used to describe linear equations, keep track of the coefficients of linear transformations and to record data that depend on multiple parameters. Matrices are described by the field of _____ theory.

a. Compression
c. Double counting
b. Coherent
d. Matrix

8. _____ is the mathematical operation of scaling one number by another. It is one of the four basic operations in elementary arithmetic.

Chapter 11. MATRICES AND MARKOV CHAINS

_____ is defined for whole numbers in terms of repeated addition; for example, 4 multiplied by 3 can be calculated by adding 3 copies of 4 together:

$$4 + 4 + 4 = 12.$$

_____ of rational numbers and real numbers is defined by systematic generalization of this basic idea.

a. The number 0 is even.
c. Highest common factor

b. Least common multiple
d. Multiplication

9. In mathematics, the term _____ has several different important meanings:

- An _____ is an equality that remains true regardless of the values of any variables that appear within it, to distinguish it from an equality which is true under more particular conditions. For this, the 'triple bar' symbol ≡ is sometimes used.
- In algebra, an _____ or _____ element of a set S with a binary operation Â· is an element e that, when combined with any element x of S, produces that same x. That is, eÂ·x = xÂ·e = x for all x in S.
    - The _____ function from a set S to itself, often denoted id or id_S, s the function such that i = x for all x in S. This function serves as the _____ element in the set of all functions from S to itself with respect to function composition.
    - In linear algebra, the _____ matrix of size n is the n-by-n square matrix with ones on the main diagonal and zeros elsewhere. This matrix serves as the _____ with respect to matrix multiplication.

A common example of the first meaning is the trigonometric _____

$$\sin^2 \theta + \cos^2 \theta = 1$$

which is true for all real values of θ, as opposed to

$$\cos \theta = 1,$$

which is true only for some values of θ, not all. For example, the latter equation is true when $\theta = 0$, false when $\theta = 2$

The concepts of 'additive _____' and 'multiplicative _____' are central to the Peano axioms. The number 0 is the 'additive _____' for integers, real numbers, and complex numbers. For the real numbers, for all $a \in \mathbb{R}$,

$$0 + a = a,$$

$$a + 0 = a, \text{ and}$$

$$0 + 0 = 0.$$

Similarly, The number 1 is the 'multiplicative _____' for integers, real numbers, and complex numbers.

   a. Identity   b. Action
   c. ARIA   d. Intersection

10.   In linear algebra, the _____ or unit matrix of size n is the n-by-n square matrix with ones on the main diagonal and zeros elsewhere. It is denoted by I_n, or simply by I if the size is immaterial or can be trivially determined by the context. (In some fields, such as quantum mechanics, the _____ is denoted by a boldface one, 1; otherwise it is identical to I.)
   a. Unital   b. Identity matrix
   c. Arity   d. Associativity

11.   In mathematics, _____ is the operation of multiplying a matrix with either a scalar or another matrix

This is the most often used and most important way to multiply matrices.

   a. Logarithmic norm   b. Jordan matrix
   c. Matrix calculus   d. Matrix multiplication

12.   _____ is the branch of physics concerned with the behaviour of physical bodies when subjected to forces or displacements, and the subsequent effect of the bodies on their environment. The discipline has its roots in several ancient civilizations. During the early modern period, scientists such as Galileo, Kepler, and especially Newton, laid the foundation for what is now known as classical _____.
   a. 120-cell   b. Parallel axes rule
   c. 1-center problem   d. Mechanics

13.   In physics, a _____ (plural: quanta) is an indivisible entity of a quantity that has the same units as the Planck constant and is related to both energy and momentum of elementary particles of matter (called fermions) and of photons and other bosons. The word comes from the Latin 'quantus,' for 'how much.' Behind this, one finds the fundamental notion that a physical property may be 'quantized', referred to as 'quantization'. This means that the magnitude can take on only certain discrete numerical values, rather than any value, at least within a range.
   a. Quantum numbers   b. Wigner-Eckart theorem
   c. Quantum   d. Heisenberg picture

Chapter 11. MATRICES AND MARKOV CHAINS

14. _____ is a set of principles underlying the most fundamental known description of all physical systems; it is more fundamental than classical mechanics and classical field theory. Notable amongst these principles are both a dual wave-like and particle-like behavior of matter and radiation, and prediction of probabilities in situations where classical physics predicts certainties. Classical physics can be derived as a good approximation to quantum physics, typically in circumstances with large numbers of particles.
   a. Fock space
   b. Probability amplitude
   c. Quantum mechanics
   d. Quantum

15. In linear algebra, _____ is a version of Gaussian elimination that puts zeros both above and below each pivot element as it goes from the top row of the given matrix to the bottom. In other words, _____ brings a matrix to reduced row echelon form, whereas Gaussian elimination takes it only as far as row echelon form. Every matrix has a reduced row echelon form, and this algorithm is guaranteed to produce it.
   a. Lax equivalence theorem
   b. Conservation form
   c. Gauss-Jordan elimination
   d. Spheroidal wave functions

16. A _____ is a device for performing mathematical calculations, distinguished from a computer by having a limited problem solving ability and an interface optimized for interactive calculation rather than programming. _____s can be hardware or software, and mechanical or electronic, and are often built into devices such as PDAs or mobile phones.

Modern electronic _____s are generally small, digital, and usually inexpensive.

   a. Calculator
   b. 2-3 heap
   c. 120-cell
   d. 1-center problem

17. A _____ typically refers to a class of handheld calculators that are capable of plotting graphs, solving simultaneous equations, and performing numerous other tasks with variables. Most popular _____s are also programmable, allowing the user to create customized programs, typically for scientific/engineering and education applications. Due to their large displays intended for graphing, they can also accommodate several lines of text and calculations at a time.
   a. Bump mapping
   b. Genus
   c. Graphing calculator
   d. Support vector machines

18. In mathematics, more particularly in functional analysis, differential topology, and geometric measure theory, a _____ in the sense of Georges de Rham is a functional on the space of compactly supported differential k-forms, on a smooth manifold M. Formally currents behave like Schwartz distributions on a space of differential forms. In a geometric sense they can represent quite singular versions of submanifolds: Dirac delta functions or even multipoles spread out along subsets of M.
   a. Convex and concave
   b. Convex analysis
   c. Continuous-time Markov process
   d. K-current

19. In mathematics, a stochastic matrix, probability matrix, or _____ is used to describe the transitions of a Markov chain. It has found use in probability theory, statistics and linear algebra, as well as computer science. There are several different definitions and types of stochastic matrices;

   A right stochastic matrix is a square matrix each of whose rows consists of nonnegative real numbers, with each row summing to 1.

a. Sylvester matrix
c. Hessenberg matrix
b. Pick matrix
d. Transition matrix

20. _____ is the likelihood or chance that something is the case or will happen. Theoretical _____ is used extensively in areas such as statistics, mathematics, science and philosophy to draw conclusions about the likelihood of potential events and the underlying mechanics of complex systems.

The word _____ does not have a consistent direct definition.

a. Standardized moment
c. Statistical significance
b. Discrete random variable
d. Probability

21. A _____ is an algebraic equation in which each term is either a constant or the product of a constant and a single variable. _____s can have one, two, three or more variables.

_____s occur with great regularity in applied mathematics.

a. Quadratic equation
c. Difference of two squares
b. Quartic equation
d. Linear equation

22. In mathematics and physics, there are a _____ number of topics named in honor of Leonhard Euler . As well, many of these topics include their own unique function, equation, formula, identity, number, or other mathematical entity. Unfortunately however, many of these entities have been given simple names like Euler's function, Euler's equation, and Euler's formula, which are further confused by variations of the 'Euler'-prefix Overall though, Euler's work touched upon so many fields that he is often the earliest written reference on a given matter.

a. List of mathematical knots and links
c. List of integrals of logarithmic functions
b. Large
d. List of trigonometry topics

Chapter 12. LINEAR PROGRAMMING

1. In mathematics, _____ and undefined are used to explain whether or not expressions have meaningful, sensible, and unambiguous values. Not all branches of mathematics come to the same conclusion.

The following expressions are undefined in all contexts, but remarks in the analysis section may apply.

   a. LHS
   b. Plugging in
   c. Toy model
   d. Defined

2. In linear algebra, _____ is a version of Gaussian elimination that puts zeros both above and below each pivot element as it goes from the top row of the given matrix to the bottom. In other words, _____ brings a matrix to reduced row echelon form, whereas Gaussian elimination takes it only as far as row echelon form. Every matrix has a reduced row echelon form, and this algorithm is guaranteed to produce it.

   a. Spheroidal wave functions
   b. Conservation form
   c. Lax equivalence theorem
   d. Gauss-Jordan elimination

3. In mathematics, _____ is a technique for optimization of a linear objective function, subject to linear equality and linear inequality constraints. Informally, _____ determines the way to achieve the best outcome in a given mathematical model given some list of requirements represented as linear equations.

More formally, given a polytope, and a real-valued affine function

$$f(x_1, x_2, \ldots, x_n) = c_1 x_1 + c_2 x_2 + \cdots + c_n x_n + d$$

defined on this polytope, a _____ method will find a point in the polytope where this function has the smallest value.

   a. Lin-Kernighan
   b. Linear programming
   c. Linear programming relaxation
   d. Descent direction

4. In mathematics, a _____, named after Andrey Markov, is a stochastic process with the Markov property. Having the Markov property means that, given the present state, future states are independent of the past states. In other words, the description of the present state fully captures all the information that could influence the future evolution of the process. Future states will be reached through a probabilistic process instead of a deterministic one.

   a. Law of Truly Large Numbers
   b. Possibility theory
   c. Variance-to-mean ratio
   d. Markov chain

5. In mathematics, an _____ is a statement about the relative size or order of two objects, or about whether they are the same or not

   - The notation a < b means that a is less than b.
   - The notation a > b means that a is greater than b.
   - The notation a ≠ b means that a is not equal to b, but does not say that one is bigger than the other or even that they can be compared in size.

In all these cases, a is not equal to b, hence, '_____'.

Chapter 12. LINEAR PROGRAMMING

These relations are known as strict _____

- The notation a ≤ b means that a is less than or equal to b;
- The notation a ≥ b means that a is greater than or equal to b;

An additional use of the notation is to show that one quantity is much greater than another, normally by several orders of magnitude.

- The notation a << b means that a is much less than b.
- The notation a >> b means that a is much greater than b.

If the sense of the _____ is the same for all values of the variables for which its members are defined, then the _____ is called an 'absolute' or 'unconditional' _____. If the sense of an _____ holds only for certain values of the variables involved, but is reversed or destroyed for other values of the variables, it is called a conditional _____.

An _____ may appear unsolvable because it only states whether a number is larger or smaller than another number; but it is possible to apply the same operations for equalities to inequalities. For example, to find x for the _____ 10x > 23 one would divide 23 by 10.

a. A posteriori
b. Inequality
c. A Mathematical Theory of Communication
d. A chemical equation

6. A set S of real numbers is called _____ from above if there is a real number k such that k ≥ s for all s in S. The number k is called an upper bound of S. The terms _____ from below and lower bound are similarly defined.
a. Derivative algebra
b. Harmonic series
c. Descent
d. Bounded

7. A _____ is a device for performing mathematical calculations, distinguished from a computer by having a limited problem solving ability and an interface optimized for interactive calculation rather than programming. _____s can be hardware or software, and mechanical or electronic, and are often built into devices such as PDAs or mobile phones.

Modern electronic _____s are generally small, digital, and usually inexpensive.

a. 120-cell
b. Calculator
c. 1-center problem
d. 2-3 heap

8. A _____ typically refers to a class of handheld calculators that are capable of plotting graphs, solving simultaneous equations, and performing numerous other tasks with variables. Most popular _____s are also programmable, allowing the user to create customized programs, typically for scientific/engineering and education applications. Due to their large displays intended for graphing, they can also accommodate several lines of text and calculations at a time.
a. Genus
b. Support vector machines
c. Bump mapping
d. Graphing calculator

Chapter 12. LINEAR PROGRAMMING

9. In mathematics, a _____ is a condition that a solution to an optimization problem must satisfy. There are two types of _____s: equality _____s and inequality _____s. The set of solutions that satisfy all _____s is called the feasible set.
   a. Foci
   b. Decidable
   c. Concurrent
   d. Constraint

10. _____ and independent variables refer to values that change in relationship to each other. The _____ are those that are observed to change in response to the independent variables. The independent variables are those that are deliberately manipulated to invoke a change in the _____.
    a. Steiner system
    b. Dependent variables
    c. Yates analysis
    d. Round robin test

11. _____ is a part of mathematics concerned with questions of size, shape, and relative position of figures and with properties of space. _____ is one of the oldest sciences. Initially a body of practical knowledge concerning lengths, areas, and volumes, in the third century BC _____ was put into an axiomatic form by Euclid, whose treatment--Euclidean _____--set a standard for many centuries to follow.
    a. 1-center problem
    b. 2-3 heap
    c. 120-cell
    d. Geometry

12. Dependent variables and _____ refer to values that change in relationship to each other. The dependent variables are those that are observed to change in response to the _____. The _____ are those that are deliberately manipulated to invoke a change in the dependent variables.
    a. Independent variables
    b. Operational confound
    c. One-factor-at-a-time method
    d. Experimental design diagram

13. A _____ is an abstract model that uses mathematical language to describe the behavior of a system. Eykhoff defined a _____ as 'a representation of the essential aspects of an existing system which presents knowledge of that system in usable form'.
    a. Rata Die
    b. Metaheuristic
    c. Mathematical model
    d. Total least squares

14. An _____ is a tree data structure in which each internal node has up to eight children. _____s are most often used to partition a three dimensional space by recursively subdividing it into eight octants. _____s are the three-dimensional analog of quadtrees.
    a. External node
    b. Adaptive k-d tree
    c. Interval tree
    d. Octree

15. _____ is a quantity expressing the two-dimensional size of a defined part of a surface, typically a region bounded by a closed curve. The term surface _____ refers to the total _____ of the exposed surface of a 3-dimensional solid, such as the sum of the _____s of the exposed sides of a polyhedron. _____ is an important invariant in the differential geometry of surfaces.
    a. A Mathematical Theory of Communication
    b. Area
    c. A posteriori
    d. A chemical equation

16. The mathematical concept of a _____ expresses the intuitive idea of deterministic dependence between two quantities, one of which is viewed as primary and the other as secondary. A _____ then is a way to associate a unique output for each input of a specified type, for example, a real number or an element of a given set.
   a. Grill
   b. Function
   c. Coherent
   d. Going up

ANSWER KEY

Chapter 1
1. c	2. d	3. b	4. a	5. a	6. d	7. d	8. a	9. c	10. d
11. d	12. c	13. a	14. d	15. b	16. b	17. a	18. a	19. d	20. d
21. c	22. d	23. b	24. b	25. d	26. a	27. d	28. b	29. d	30. d
31. d	32. c	33. d	34. d	35. a	36. b	37. d	38. d	39. d	40. d
41. d	42. d	43. b	44. b	45. a	46. a	47. d	48. d	49. a	50. c
51. d	52. c	53. d	54. d	55. a	56. d	57. b	58. d	59. a	60. c
61. b	62. b	63. d	64. d	65. c	66. b	67. d	68. d	69. b	70. a
71. b	72. b								

Chapter 2
1. d	2. d	3. d	4. d	5. d	6. d	7. b	8. b	9. d	10. a
11. c	12. d	13. b	14. d	15. a	16. c	17. b	18. d	19. c	20. d
21. b	22. d	23. d	24. b	25. d	26. d	27. c	28. d	29. d	30. d
31. d	32. d	33. d	34. b	35. c	36. c	37. c	38. b	39. b	40. a
41. d	42. d	43. c	44. b	45. d	46. b				

Chapter 3
1. d	2. a	3. b	4. d	5. c	6. b	7. a	8. c	9. d	10. a
11. d	12. d	13. d	14. d	15. d	16. b	17. c	18. b	19. c	20. d
21. d	22. b	23. b	24. d	25. d	26. a	27. b	28. d	29. a	30. c
31. d	32. d	33. d	34. c	35. d	36. d	37. d	38. d	39. a	40. d
41. b									

Chapter 4
1. d	2. d	3. c	4. c	5. c	6. b	7. a	8. d	9. b	10. d
11. c	12. a	13. d	14. a	15. d	16. d	17. d	18. d	19. d	20. d
21. d	22. a	23. d	24. d	25. a	26. c	27. d	28. d	29. d	30. d
31. c	32. d	33. c	34. d	35. b	36. c	37. d	38. d	39. d	40. b
41. d	42. d	43. d	44. d	45. d	46. d	47. a	48. d	49. d	50. d
51. a	52. d	53. d	54. a	55. a	56. d	57. c			

Chapter 5
1. d	2. a	3. a	4. b	5. d	6. d	7. d	8. a	9. d	10. d
11. b	12. d	13. d	14. a	15. c	16. b	17. b	18. d	19. a	20. d
21. d	22. b								

Chapter 6
1. d	2. b	3. d	4. d	5. a	6. d	7. c	8. d	9. b

Chapter 7
1. b	2. d	3. c	4. d	5. d	6. c	7. d	8. d	9. c	10. a
11. d	12. b	13. d	14. d	15. a	16. d	17. c	18. c	19. b	20. c
21. b	22. d	23. d	24. d	25. c	26. d	27. d	28. b	29. a	30. a
31. a	32. b	33. d	34. d	35. d					

Chapter 8

1. b	2. a	3. d	4. d	5. c	6. a	7. d	8. d	9. b	10. d
11. b	12. d	13. d	14. c	15. d	16. d	17. b	18. b	19. b	20. d
21. c	22. d	23. d	24. d	25. b	26. d	27. d	28. d	29. d	30. c
31. d	32. b	33. d	34. d	35. d	36. d	37. c	38. b	39. d	40. c
41. d	42. d	43. d	44. a	45. b	46. d	47. d	48. d	49. b	50. d
51. d	52. c	53. a	54. c	55. d	56. c	57. a	58. d	59. d	60. b
61. d	62. b	63. d	64. b	65. a	66. d	67. d	68. d	69. d	70. d
71. a	72. c	73. d	74. d	75. c	76. a	77. d	78. d	79. a	80. d

Chapter 9

1. d	2. d	3. d	4. d	5. b	6. a	7. a	8. a	9. a	10. c
11. c	12. b	13. b	14. d	15. b	16. d	17. a	18. a	19. d	20. d
21. a	22. d	23. c	24. a	25. d	26. d	27. c	28. c	29. a	30. b
31. c	32. a	33. d	34. c						

Chapter 10

1. d	2. b	3. d	4. d	5. c	6. b	7. d	8. d	9. a	10. b
11. c	12. d	13. a	14. c	15. b	16. d	17. d	18. c	19. a	20. d
21. d	22. a	23. d	24. d	25. a	26. d	27. a	28. c	29. d	30. b
31. d	32. a	33. d	34. d	35. d	36. d				

Chapter 11

1. a	2. b	3. d	4. d	5. d	6. a	7. d	8. d	9. a	10. b
11. d	12. d	13. c	14. c	15. c	16. a	17. c	18. d	19. d	20. d
21. d	22. b								

Chapter 12

1. d	2. d	3. b	4. d	5. b	6. d	7. b	8. d	9. d	10. b
11. d	12. a	13. c	14. d	15. b	16. b				

www.ingramcontent.com/pod-product-compliance
Lightning Source LLC
Chambersburg PA
CBHW081845230426
43669CB00018B/2827